M000281469

Hunting, Fishing and Family:
From the Hills of West Virginia

HUNTING, FISHING AND FAMILY

FROM THE HILLS OF WEST VIRGINIA

CHRIS ELLIS

Quarrier Press
Charleston, WV

Quarrier Press
Charleston, WV

All articles were originally published in *The Herald Dispatch* in Huntington, and the *Register-Herald* in Beckley, West Virginia. Reprinted with permission.

Book and cover design: Mark S. Phillips

ISBN 10: 1-942294-15-8
ISBN 13: 978-1-942294-15-3

10 9 8 7 6 5 4 3 2 1

Printed in the United States of America

Distributed by:

West Virginia Book Co.
1125 Central Ave.
Charleston, WV 25302
www.wvbookco.com

DEDICATION

I dedicate this book to all those who took the time to teach me the art of outdoor pursuits—Pop, Grandad, Mr. Monk. May I always hear your voices in the rustle of the wind, in the murmur of water over rocks and in the stillness of a perfect autumn morning.

For Tina—LOVE.

TABLE ⟨OF⟩ CONTENTS

INTRODUCTION

There's no sound like a coal train moving up a river valley. The rumble, as the 100-car train struggles to pull the grade, gives you the impression the mountains are mourning the erosion that birthed them. There's no sound like the lonesome bawl of a hound splitting the darkness as he trails a raccoon along a ragged ridge. And there's no sound that can compare to the words of a grandfather explaining how to bait a hook or call in a turkey.

The Scots-Irish who settled the Allegheny Mountains were hardy, independent, clannish, family-loving immigrants who birthed the hillbilly—mountain-folk—lifestyle that's eternally linked to the Mountain State. West Virginians don't just live in the hills, we're part of 'em. We're an integral piece of a temperate forest habitat within an alpine/montane ecosystem, where fishing, hunting, stringing beans with Grandma, and learning the outdoors from Grandpa, are everyday life.

You can't *imagine* the life of a hillbilly and understand his relationship with the outdoors. You can't watch a documentary and grasp his fundamental, spiritual-like connection to the wilderness he lives in. And, until now, you could not read a book and learn how vital the interaction with nature is to the spirit of a born-and-raised West Virginian.

Hunting, Fishing and Family: From the Hills of West Virginia is a collection of short newspaper articles written by a hillbilly who is one of the most complete outdoorsmen I know. Chris Ellis and I have shared outside adventures across West Virginia and the world; he can skin a buck and run a trot-line; and he can read a river with the devoted skill of a reverend reciting a sermon. But most importantly, Chris Ellis can tell stories, stories that reflect the hillbilly that's inside him and thousands like him. *Hunting, Fishing and Family: From the Hills of West Virginia* will give you a glimpse—a lick of the spoon if you will—of the emotional connection true hillbillies have to everything that's *wild and wonderful.*

My father, another hillbilly outdoorsman who now treads hunting grounds and wades streams on a much higher plane, used to call me every Sunday. After asking about the kids, the garden and the dogs, he'd say, "I read Chris's story in the newspaper today. It reminded me of..." and he'd go on to tell me about some outdoor experience from his or my youth. And that is the mark of a truly good story; it brings back a memory or drives you to create new ones.

I don't fish much anymore, I gave up coon hunting for a normal family life, and Grandpa's words were spoken to me nearly a half-century ago. But train whistles, hound dogs, and *Hunting, Fishing and Family: From the Hills of West Virginia* help keep those memories—memories that are hooked to something deep and running hard—as crisp, refreshing, and vital to my well-being, as a drink from a cool mountain stream.

Richard Mann
Outdoor Writer/Hillbilly
www.empty-cases.com

GROWING UP, UP ELK RIVER

Growing up on the Elk River provided me with continuous outdoor opportunities. Early spring meant big fish and therefore big bait would need to be found. Traps were set and tended so that bait was on hand when the word at the barbershop shop was, "Big bass are hitting in the still pools of the river."

Early summertime is when the fishing is easy and the bait is not too critical and artificial soft plastic baits were preferred in the shoals and riffles. Each season caused my mind to wander and my body to fill with excitement of what was coming next.

It is that anticipation that perhaps caused my lifelong passion of outdoor writings and great story telling. It is in the same four walls of the local barber shop where the fish tales were spoken, and you could find magazines filled with stories of wild critters.

Waiting your turn for the chair was never a boring endeavor. With hunting and fishing stories being told by the men and with a stack of magazines to flip through on the table, I was in paradise.

I treated the visit to the barbershop like a freshman science student treats their first biology class in college. I was ready and eager to learn.

It was that simple exercise of getting a haircut and

listening to old men talk and debate everything from the best lure for stock trout, best rifle load for deer or to pass around a tailgate picture of a big deer they took that solidified my longing to dedicate my vocation to outdoor pursuits.

Today, I am still learning. As long as my body and mind keep up with the excitement and thrill of going afield, I plan to continue long into the future.

GRANDFATHER'S DAY

Grandad was a fisherman. He was simply more than someone who liked to fish. A person who likes to fish, for example, may wake up on a Saturday morning and decide a day on the water sounds nice. But a fisherman works all week readying his tackle and gear so that by Saturday, they have the utmost opportunity to catch fish. Sure, someone who likes to fish may throw one lure with the perfect cast and snag a fish. But a fisherman has the knowledge and experience to do it time after time.

After work on Friday, Grandad would drive to local creeks to catch bait. Whether it was seining for minnow and hellgrammites or his personal favorite, crawdads, he didn't come home until he had enough bait for the fishing outing. His specialty was crawling up the creeks at night with the use of a carbide lamp to find molting crawfish, soft-shelled crawdads. He knew the value of a handful of soft-shells was worth the aggravation and loss of sleep. He knew when placed on the right bait hook and with the right amount of weight, he could lure a smallmouth into striking. And he proved it often.

Although I wasn't there, I remember the story of the big smallmouth Grandad hooked and landed from under a downed tree. A tree had fallen from the bank

3

and the top of the tree was resting on the bottom of the creek. The creek's current pushed against the tree causing a circling eddy, making a dandy spot for a fish to hide. It also made for a tough place to cast and to retrieve your bait without getting tangled up.

Grandad had studied the hole and knew how to read water so he waited for the conditions to be just right. With the aid of a simply perfect soft-shell craw, a spool of light line as to not spook the fish, and a tiny weight, he cast the rig up under the sunken tree. As the bait slowly began to sink under the log, he flipped the reel's bail so that the creek's current could push the bait naturally.

Once the bait reached the bottom, he closed the reel's bail and placed his finger on the line to get a better feel for when the fish picked up the soft-shell. With a thump felt on the line, he let the trophy run up stream before he set the hook. If he set it too soon, he would run the risk of getting tangled in the wooden debris and lose the fish. When he felt enough distance was reached and he was in the clear, he set the hook and the light-line battle between fish and man was on.

Grandad took me fishing. He was a mentor that took the time to teach me how to fish and what it means to become a fisherman. Happy Father's Day Grandad. I think of you daily and I take your great-grandson fishing often so that he too, may hear your words.

ELK

Being from West Virginia, I have always felt that elk and I were somehow connected. As strange as that may seem, perhaps growing up on the Elk River near Elkview may have caused this feeling. I often wondered why so many places in our home state had the word "elk" in their name.

A quick glance at WVDNR's Elk Management Plan under the heading of Historical Overview of Elk In West Virginia sheds some light. Historically, elk were common throughout most of the contiguous 48 states, including all of West Virginia. Large numbers were found in the Ohio and Kanawha river valleys and the higher mountain regions.

Elk provided an important source for food, shelter and clothing for American Indians and early settlers.

Evidence of their distribution throughout the state is illustrated by the widespread use of elk in place names. However, it should also be noted that early explorers often used the word "elk" to describe white-tailed deer.

Elk population densities declined in West Virginia throughout the 1800s. Subsistence hunting, market hunting and wide scale timbering all contributed to the decline of the elk. By the late 1800s, elk were completely eliminated from West Virginia, with the last native elk records being reported from the headwaters of the Cheat River in Pocahontas County in 1873 and the Webster Springs area in 1875.

My curiosity of the animal and its behavior has triggered my desire to hunt elk ever since I was a child. And this past week, I acted upon that desire in the Rocky Mountains. In the massive mountainsides and valleys of the west, elk could be heard bugling and it was simply up to your lungs and legs to decide if you wanted to go in pursuit of the majestic animal.

It was on one of those high elevation mountainsides, the story of my hunt began. After a long walk up the steep slope, I stopped to rest my overworked lungs and legs. With binoculars in hand, I searched the pine trees for movement. In the thin mountain air, the bull's bugle rang out across the rugged landscape.

I heard him but I could not see him. I decided to walk parallel to the hillside to see if perhaps I could find him in the timber. Again, he bugled.

As I studied the steep terrain, I caught movement to my right—cow elk. The cow elk was feeding along a narrow game trail carved out amongst rocks, scrub brush and pines. He bugled again only this time to my calls. As I studied each opening, more and more cows could be seen. In addition, I spotted some younger bulls sparring below the herd in hopes to impress the females. He bugled again from his shady hiding spot.

After nearly an hour of not moving and scanning the mountain rising high before me, he stepped out to better hear my calls. With the report of my rifle echoing across the rugged canyons, I began my slow, steep climb uphill towards the bull elk.

As I reached down to touch his antlers, I turned and looked at the view stretching as far as the eye could see before me. It was if I was sitting on top of the world. My thoughts turned back to my home and the recent reintroduction of elk to our state. Perhaps one day in the near future, a hunter will hear the bugle of a bull elk but only this time, touch his antlers in the Mountain State.

MOTHER'S DAY STORY

Many years ago, a member of my hunting family moved to new grounds and joined another party. This particular member played an important role for us.

I didn't realize how much of a role she played until recently; when I found myself poorly trying to fill her position. She handled the responsibilities with such ease that I often overlooked her efforts and only now have I begun to appreciate it completely.

The role left vacant would seem to most to be that of a parental position or one that as you matured, would no longer be required. It is true I never saw this person shoot a deer, bear, squirrel, or well anything, for that matter. But like all successful outings, the conquest overshadows the behind the scenes work.

I have not seen or met anyone who could prepare more thoroughly for an adventure. It did not matter whether it was a weekend in Ritchie County at a deer camp or a 10-day jaunt in the backcountry; things were in order and well planned out. In the down time, routine maintenance and repair of our clothing, sleeping bags, and day packs were seen as standard operating procedures in order to keep the gear readied for a moment's notice.

The meals were prepared well in advance so that

even cold, tired, worn out woodsmen would have homemade meals instead of eating beanie-weenies and snack cakes that her boys would have packed if left on their own. Even on next to no notice, the truck could be packed and readied as if she had been given two-weeks' notice.

She had an uncanny ability to predict arrival and departure times for our hunts. We often left without an estimated return time and I would always be amazed how she would know exactly when we would return and have something warm for us and a place to sit at her table so we could tell her our grand tales. Even more amazing is how she would not complain but find pride in unpacking and readying the gear for the next trip even if it was the following morning.

The sad reality is, she will never be replaced. In fact, the job posting was removed many years ago and only fond childhood memories exist. I miss you Mom. I will make sure I pack your grandson a raincoat, make sure he stays warm, and take the time to listen to his tales of grand adventures. I know you will hear him too.

THE TURKEY OPENER

My boots are beside the door. My old turkey vest has been organized and my calls are tuned, chalked, and placed in their proper pocket. I have experimented with so many loads for my muzzleloading shotgun that I can recite the fine attributes of how a particular over-powder wad will affect shot patterns at 35 yards. I am obsessed.

Spring Gobbler season starts tomorrow and many of us will take the predawn march atop a high ridge to listen for the turkeys announcing to the world that it is dawn. Maybe a barred owl will start the chorus off with a hoot or an anxious young gobbler will try and force his way into daylight by gobbling first.

Anyhow, the game is the same year after year. The game is all about the girls. Like a bunch of teenage boys, the gobblers are all trying to figure out where the girls are heading. As the womenfolk begin to wake up on their tree limb roosts and make a few little morning sighs, the gobblers are all ears listening to them just in case they spill the beans as to where the local hang out is going to be this particular morning.

The young gobblers holler as loud as possible from their limbs knowing that once their feet hit the ground, the older gobblers will be watching them and have no problem using brute force to put them back in their pecking order. Even old mature gobblers can't handle the girls and begin to act like teenagers. In fact, an old gobbler who is usually well mannered and very reserved now begins to run his mouth and simply act like a crazed boy who drank too much Mountain Dew. The early morning ritual of the spring season is always interesting, to say the least, and I don't plan on giving up my front row seat anytime soon.

The season only lasts four weeks and it is our rare opportunity to get a chance to live amongst turkeys. We might get the chance to fool an old gobbler or we may send the whole flock running into an adjacent county. The sport is challenging, by design for the conservation of the birds. This makes the dressing and mash potatoes taste even better when the old bird is served on Sunday's best china one memorable afternoon.

It is now time to hunt the grand gobbler on his terms, on his turf. If you are so lucky to call him into shotgun range and are successful, take a moment or two to reflect on your accomplishment. It will be a moment you will not forget.

NATIVE BROOKIES

I have a certain connection to a fish. I know that sounds a little odd, but let me explain.

In my youth, I had plenty of influence that pointed me down the path of outdoor pursuits. From camping, cooking outdoors, hiking and hunting and fishing—there was always someone around to ask the tough questions that came from being a kid. A curious mind and an absolute willingness to learn how to survive and prosper made growing up wonderful for me. I wanted to learn how to paddle a canoe, set a trap, catch a catfish, cook a meal over fire, set up a tent—everything. I was and still am a sponge for information on how to do things better or become a more efficient sportsman. It was in this quest that I was introduced to a fish.

One of my greatest mentors introduced me to the trout on a crisp late spring morning in Pocahontas County.

Knowing that I loved to fish, he sent his son and I on a mission. While he was setting up camp, he pointed us to a valley with a tiny creek pushing water down the hill very quickly. And in that little cold creek, there were trout. Not just any trout, but the trout he called natives.

After several casts in a small pool, I learned quickly that these were certainly not like stocked trout. These little fish were wary and liked to hide in shadowy places. As I crawled up slowly and discreetly to the next little pool, I casted as lightly as I could into the next run.

As soon as my bug hit the water, a trout like I have never seen before absolutely attacked the bait. A massive strike was met with a little tussle and shortly after I held in my hands—a native brook trout. It was love at first sight.

About the native brook trout from our WVDNR— the brook trout is the only trout species native to West Virginia streams. They live and reproduce in only the coldest and purest of our mountain streams. These streams are generally less than 15 feet wide, well shaded, and have numerous pools. Although these streams often support large numbers of brook trout, the trout tend to be small and average five to six inches in length and seldom exceed 10 inches.

A dark green back covered with lighter worm-shaped markings, bluish sides and a pink to scarlet belly characterizes brook trout. The sides of the trout are profusely sprinkled with yellow spots, interspersed with red ones. The lower fins are orange-red with a distinctive white stripe on the front edge.

Given its beauty and the fact that the brook trout is our only native trout, it's no wonder that in 1973 it was selected to be the official state fish.

While there are 500 miles of native trout streams in West Virginia, the streams are small and represent only two percent of the total miles of stream in the state.

SUMMER AT POP'S

Every summer of my youth, my brother and I would spend a week with our grandparents. Most often the weather would be hot and humid causing towering clouds to build in the sky and thunder to be heard off in the distance. Like clockwork, the afternoon winds would shift, bringing a downpour to the parched ground. Then the storm would exit as quickly as it arrived, leaving mud puddles and more humidity behind.

Having two boys visit your house bouncing off the walls to do something besides sweat and watch grandma cook was cause for a plan.

Perhaps it was his rural upbringing, his passion for the sporting lifestyle or his time in the Army that gave him the talent of planning. I am not sure. But what I am sure of is that, he was a master at plans. He could lay out an itinerary for us boys that caused so much excitement we found it hard to sleep the night before.

His plan to beat the heat and chill the rambunctious behavior of two adolescent grandchildren was to take us camping. He had done his homework and found a shady patch of ground resting beside a deep hole in the creek. Above and below the hole of water were ankle-deep riffles. With a glorious setting before us, he crafted daily activities to keep us cool and our minds occupied.

We would catch crawdads in the riffles in the morning, swim in the heat of the day, run a trotline across the pool in the evening and listen and learn the sounds of night animals while feeling the warmth and protection from a campfire at night.

We were so waterlogged and beat from his prearranged activities that we fell into our cots and slept peacefully through the night. We would awake to smell of bacon being fried and toast crisping from the embers left smoldering in the fire ring.

Once our bodies were refueled, he took the enthusiasm of a new day to teach us important skills he felt were needed to prosper in the outdoors. All the previous days' worth of activities were used as stepping-stones in our education. For example, he had let us swim in the creek's pool as practice and to gauge our skill. Once he felt comfortable with our swimming ability, we learned to paddle a canoe in a straight line without tipping it over. Once we mastered that, he taught us to run a trotline—using the bait we caught in the riffles we had fish to learn how to scale, fillet and cook for supper.

It's in that transitional time of a summer day, when we humans slow down and the night creatures awaken from their siestas, when life's reflections can easily slip into our memories. Mine are generally of him and his passion for the arts of outdoor pursuits.

Its summertime; when the living and memories come easy.

COUSIN'S TROUT

The first look at the creek indicated it was in great shape for a hot, August day. As we pulled the vehicle off the road on a gravel wide spot, the boys jumped out and hurredly started to ready their gear. For passersby, we must have looked odd and somewhat like a NASCAR pit crew running around the car.

After a car ride filled with big fish speak and little flies talk, it's perfectly normal to be amped up at the first hole of the fishing trip. As per the norm, I witnessed some less-than-perfect casting and some hurry-up movements. The boys were excited to say the least. Still, the creek's almost ideal water and picture-perfect run for fly-fishing should have produced at least a fish or two.

I chalked it up to excited nerves and led our band of fishermen to the next section. I chose a particular section for two reasons. The first was that it always holds trout. The second reason was that it required a little bit of hike and an upstream walk to best cover the section of creek. I was hoping the walk would settle them down.

The casts I then witnessed were spot on. They had settled down and were really fishing hard. And yet, no fish. Only a few swats by creek minnows and the occasional no-thank-you look by a trout resting peacefully in its hole behind a rock.

We were in the middle of being skunked. At the last run in the section, I noticed the water was rising and I was starting to see leaves and sticks floating down the creek. The water was turning colors quickly from a clear green to a cloudy brown.

We decided to drive towards the upper section of creek in hopes of cleaner waters. None was to be found. I pulled the truck over at a wide spot beside a bridge crossing the now dirty water creek. As we stepped out one in our group said loudly, "One more cast!" As the rest of us put away our fishing gear and began the process of turning from fishermen to normal people, I witnessed something truly remarkable. The last remaining fisherman in our group was standing knee deep in cloudy water holding on to a bent rod too nervous to even speak. At the end of his line, after a swift water battle, was a prized fish by anyone's standards.

He had cast, fought and landed a trophy trout. His "one more cast" approach to a rainout day had yielded a trout and one heck of a fish tale. A fish tale we won't soon forget.

SHILOH HUNTING DOG

The other day my fourth-grade daughter Emma asked me to help her with her homework. We found a quiet corner of the house and she began to read a book. I realized I might enjoy it as well. The book was entitled *Shiloh*, written by Phyllis Reynolds Naylor.

Shiloh is a beagle dog that 11 year-old Marty finds and desperately wants to keep. The story takes place in a small West Virginia community named Friendly, high above the banks of the Ohio River. Marty goes through many of lives hard earned lessons trying to keep the dog. What my daughter was getting out of the book was not only the good-natured lessons, but the fact that Marty got to take care of a rabbit-hunting dog.

It wasn't long before she started asking questions that, as a parent, I know were coming. "Dad, isn't your buddy Buckshot from Friendly?"

"Yes." I replied.

"Didn't he used to raise hunting dogs?" Emma asked.

"Yes."

"Weren't they beagles, Daddy? Are there rabbits out at our farm?"

"Yes and Yes." I said. At this point, she knew she had me. Why is it that women and children always know how to ask me questions they know are going to stick me right in the soft spot?

By this time I am daydreaming about a perfectly sunny Saturday afternoon at the farm with just me and my kids listening to Shiloh run rabbits through the brush and how I would win the coveted *Father of the Year* award voted on by none other than a group of my peers. In fact, they might invite my family on a caribou hunt filmed for the Outdoor Channel entitled; "Take Your Kids Hunting, Don't Hunt for Your Kids." Maybe Carrie Underwood would host the show.

Interrupting my daydream Emma asked, "Dad, do you think Sandy (our household dog) needs a friend?"

Back to reality I reply, "Yes." A slight pause, a fake throat clearing and then the bomb was dropped.

"If we had a hunting dog, I would help take care of it. Daddy, can we get a beagle?"

At this point of the conversation, I did what any red-blooded West Virginia alpha male would do. I grinned, stood up, and stated proudly, "Go ask your mother."

After living a long time with a devoted hunter, my wife already had her answer planned out for this very moment. With no emotion and in a very monotone voice she said, "I don't care if you all get a hunting dog as long as I don't have to take care of it." That pretty much sealed the deal with Emma. It looks like the Ellis family is going to be getting a beagle dog named Shiloh.

Note to self, stop hanging around a guy named Buckshot from a place named Friendly.

POP'S DEER HUNTING

My grandfather was a storyteller. He could captivate an audience with childhood stories of swimming holes, pet crows or keep you hanging on the edge of your seat with a World War II account. I would sit mesmerized listening to his unhurried words and his colorful use of simple language to tell his tale. It was if I could smell the winter's wind of the Battle of the Bulge or have my very own breath taken away by the cool waters of the Cooley Hole in Irish Creek. I went on adventures with him sitting in his den that no amount of money or time could replace.

One of my favorite stories he told was about deer hunting. The story always began with the description of Army Jeeps. Every detail of the vehicle was described from the knobby tires and rough suspension to the fact that they would go anywhere and were a very effective means of transportation in rough country. He would then roll into the "in fact" part of the story, where he told of how they used them and other old military vehicles to get hunters to stands on their annual weeklong deer hunt.

Their method of hunting deer was to conduct deer drives—push deer from the thickets to open areas. These drives were well planned, well orchestrated events in which each man had a responsibility. There were deer drivers, hunters who waited for the deer called standers, a transportation unit for deer and men, butchers and even camp cooks for the week. There were a set of rules to be followed and evening sessions around a topography map to discuss strategies. It wasn't until later in life I realized my grandfather's hunting buddies were all WWII vets and the hunt was conducted like a military exercise.

My grandfather was always assigned the role of a stander. He would tell of sitting on stand for hours waiting for a glimpse of a deer and how thankful he would be to see the drivers appear walking towards him and the sounds of the old jeeps rattling up the logging trails to retrieve the cold and tired hunters.

At a time when deer were not as plentiful as today, the hunting party managed to kill deer every year and each man returned home with fresh laundered clothes and a cooler of cut and wrapped venison. The invitation to the hunt for outsiders was rare and the occasion was a highlight event for many. The annual hunt slowly vanished into history like the vets and old army jeeps.

This past week I received an invitation to a hunt in Monroe County. A group of hunters were planning an old-fashioned deer drive and with an antler-less deer tag left unfilled, I decided to accept. I had never been part of an organized deer drive and with the thoughts of my grandfather's story as vivid as if I was told it yesterday, I was thrilled to attend.

As a newcomer to the hunting party, I was assigned

the role of a stander. On a hillside overlooking a stunning snow covered landscape that only Monroe County can provide, I had a strange feeling that I had been there before. As the hunt drew to an end, I heard the sounds of a vehicle rattling across the landscape. I just knew it was an old Army truck and I pictured my grandfather smiling as he rode back to the warmth of camp.

NEW RIVER SMALLMOUTH

I almost got sick on the bus ride to the river. Between the smell of ten fishing guides, their smoke, and the exhaust from the bus my stomach was turning. I also had a case of the nerves. It had been awhile since I rowed the river and I was responsible for two anglers.

Not just their safety, I was expected to make sure they won the tournament. I was feeling old and we all knew the water was low and the rapids were rocky.

This was a rare Saturday because ten fishing guides donated their time to row twenty fishermen down the New River. The day was set up as a fishing tournament for fun, but the real reason we were there was to assist a "brother" who had been recently diagnosed with Multiple Sclerosis and whose medical bills were increasing. All the preparation, donations, and hard work was over, it was time for the 3rd annual New River Smallmouth Classic and I was honored to be there.

The bus finally arrived at the river and we all worked quickly to ready our gear and rafts before the anglers showed up. We were paired with our guests and after introductions and a little prayer for those who have gone before us, we were off. I could not help but to feel a since of awe looking down stream at ten fishing rafts.

These were men that had rowed the river for years

23

and in many people's eyes these were the best fishing guides in the business. This was indeed, a special occasion for very special person.

The anglers were competing to see who could catch the most fish and also the largest fish. The guides were competing for ribbing rights and the chance to talk junk for the next 12 months.

The river was gin clear and the fishing was good. The New River welcomed the occasion as the fish tallies added up quickly. There were several boats that landed over one hundred fish, which is truly an amazing accomplishment in an eight-hour period.

As I beached the raft at the take out, my arms and back were spent. My fishermen were tired—they had fought, landed, and released 123 fish.

MISSING HER

I am missing something. I've not misplaced anything, well I don't think. I know where my cell phone is and my wallet sits empty like most nights on the kitchen counter. My dog has not run off chasing deer and I couldn't get rid of the cat if I tried. My kids are healthy, happy, loved, and waterlogged from the lake. That's not it.

Trying to figure out what in the world I am missing, I decided to call up on old friend and spend an evening on the creek. It has been a wet spring. The local fishing report mainly consists of people waiting to go fishing to give a report.

My friend and I drove down to the same wide spot we have parked at for several years. We know every rock in the creek and have names for most of them. It is, for lack of a better term, our "home waters."

The fish did their job well, they ate and swam like they are supposed to and we quickly turned the topic from "what are they biting on?" to more pressing issues like careers, women, and other places we would like to fish. We talked of exotic places like Montana, Alaska and Welch. We decided when we retired we were both going to be fish bums and live life slow and chase sunsets across miles of trout waters. In the conversation, I remembered that I could not shake the thought that I am missing something.

Every now or then, a trout would rudely interrupt our conversation by eating our flies and we would lose track of where we were and have to start our conversation over after the normal language of fisherman like, "that was a nice take, good hook-set, pretty fish, great brown trout, looks healthy, I think we caught that same fish last fall, you? Is that a caddis fly you tied?" During one of these particular episodes, a trout hit my dry fly so hard the splash of the water startled me and in return I completely missed the fish, which then reminded me, again, I'm missing something.

An evening storm blew through. We didn't care; we just sat on a log under the canopy of a large maple tree and talked more about things we couldn't control like getting old and shared home remedies for aching knees, sore backs, and shrinking retirement funds.

After the storm and a few more casts, we walked back to the truck in the dark. On the way home I reflected on the fish, my good friend and I felt good— the kind of feeling you get from fresh mountain air and spending time outdoors. I have to admit the cold water against my legs and smell of the plants along the creek rested my soul.

As I pulled into the driveway the thought hit me again. I am missing something. The cell phone's loud ring made me jump and forced my mind back to the conscious. I answered to phone and could barely recognize my wife's voice on the other end. Cell phone coverage in Europe is sometimes sketchy and talking with her has been very difficult since she left. We talked for several minutes and we said goodbye and I hung up the phone, it hit me. She'll be home in 13 days, 11 hours, and 53 minutes. That is what I am missing.

FISHING PROMISE

I pulled into the office driveway and turned the truck off. There was a sixty percent chance of rain. The winds had already started to pick up and the poplar and maple trees were showing the bottom sides of their leaves. It was 7 o'clock in the evening and I was tired from traveling all day. I hadn't eaten since lunch and that meal had worn off several hours earlier. It wasn't looking good. I really needed to check my inbox and return a few calls that I couldn't make from the road.

I had made a promise that I would go fishing and the person I promised would be upset if I cancelled. The decision was made; I was going to keep my promise and go fishing even if it meant chasing daylight and an approaching storm.

I slammed the truck in park and was streamside in a matter of six quick steps. The water was higher than normal and a touch off color. It didn't matter; a promise is a promise. The first casts were nothing short of extremely bad and the dry fly landed hard on the surface and sank. I tried to calm down and remind myself I had more than enough time to fool a trout into a rise.

I dried the fly and with a few false casts managed to place the fly perfectly in a small eddy behind a rock. A

28

trout nosed the fly as if to say, "You'll have to do better than that you rusty old man." I quickly raised the rod and the saw the brown trout sink back to the bottom unhooked. I rolled my head around my shoulders and tried to shrug off the missed opportunity.

Above me was a set of runs and I was confident one of the runs would produce a trout. I waded quietly, watching the water's surface for a rising trout, trying to get in a position that would allow me to present the fly. A step or two more and I would have the perfect angle. I didn't see the slanted rock just below the surface because when my wading shoes attempted to gain traction on the creek's bottom, the next thing I knew I was sitting waist deep in cold water and my fly rod was floating downstream.

I gathered my gear, made a quick assessment of my injuries and retreated to the bank for a more in depth analysis. I felt like rescheduling a "mulligan" sometime in the near future. I pressed on though, keeping to my word.

I decided to hop a few holes and if I hurried I could make it to a long series of riffles just at dark. Again I rolled my head and began the process of casting my fly. The fly landed soft on the water and began to drift along the current line. By now the light was dim and the winds had calmed to welcome the night. At the end of the drift a brown trout tilted his head towards the surface and gently sipped in the fly.

The rod bent at the correct moment and the fish darted in and out of the riffle until he lay tired in my hands. I gently unhooked the fish and let him swim back into the current, back to his resting spot for the evening. I continued to fish the next two runs with similar results until the cloudy sky shadowed my fly from my vision.

The night air dampened and the fog began to settle as I rested on a rock midstream. After a long while, I readied my rod and walked back in the dark. I was content.

I had promised myself all week I would make time to go fishing. It was a promise I kept.

DAD'S ADVENTURE DAYS

When I was a child, my family would take Sunday drives. Dad called them, "adventure days." I was never informed prior to the excursion where we were going or why; I was simply a backseat passenger along for the ride and the sounds and smells open-window drives provided.

The smell of a freshly-cut hayfield, creosote-soaked railroad ties or the coolness of a river were often brought to my senses as the car's tires crunched the gravel on some backcountry road. It was on just such a road my life would change forever.

Dad pulled the car under the shade of an enormous poplar tree. My brother and I did not have the nerve to ask why we were stopping. Under the canopy of the ancient tree, stood a shack with brush and junk leaning against its tired board-and-batten siding. Barely visible from the road was a sun-bleached sign that read, "For Sale."

The property's backyard had steep banks that led to a sandy riverbank that had a river birch arching over the water. In the tree was a rusty light fixture with a bullet hole in the shade. The family watched as Dad walked the property studying every corner in great detail and not saying a word we could understand. All we heard were mumbles and grunts as his eyes fell on something he found unsightly or displeasing. After a thorough inspection, he whistled for us boys and we ran to the car in high anticipation. All he said as we left was, "We'll buy it if the price is right."

We spent every weekend for the next two summers hauling rusty trash and cutting sticky briars off the property. Everything we touched in the old house either needed repaired or destroyed depending on who was in charge of the particular project. My brother was a rip-it-out-and-start-a-fire kind of worker while Dad and I were more into saving things that gave the camp house character.

After we would complete our portion of the "project list", Dad would turn us loose to fish while he continued on his last project, which was generally to create another list for his boys.

The camp eventually was livable, at least for weekends, and we spent a good deal of time there. It's where I first learned how to paddle a canoe, caught my first trophy smallmouth bass, learned to fry frog legs, roast a pig in the ground, and discover my love of porch swings.

As life passed by, so have the camp and my father. I no longer have the joys in my life of his laughter or the smell of the Elk River from its screened-in porch.

This past week, my son and I took two days to tear down an old building at a river camp I just purchased. In all the sweat and spiders, I paused to hope he too someday will think of the camp and his father on Father's Day and hear his father's laughter in it.

THANKSGIVING

Thanksgiving is my favorite holiday. Maybe it is my love of food, family and hunting that causes my love affair to grow stronger each passing year. Or maybe it's my love of family traditions and our West Virginia culture as sportsmen that we celebrate during Thanksgiving week. How could we not love a holiday where we celebrate a day of giving thanks for the blessing of the harvest? Especially when the celebration falls in the middle of West Virginia's buck season!

The Monday of Thanksgiving week is the opener of buck season. Each hunting camp or family has their own rituals from legendary poker games to who bakes the biscuits. The high tide of tradition continues throughout the week and rolls right into the big day.

It is then that our traditions shine as we celebrate the year's harvest as friends and family say grace and give thanks over a roasted turkey. Legendary sides are prepared, football is watched, naps are taken and loved ones from long ago are remembered through words, food, and love.

At our table, Mamaw Lester's bread recipe is always tried, knowing that no one other than her could ever make it just right. But in her spirit, it is always attempted. The combination of old and new, both in recipes and family members, is what makes the meal so special.

This year, my brother and I were in a unique situation. His in-laws, as well as mine, had made plans to travel and visit other family for the holiday. That allowed the Ellis brothers to host a Thanksgiving dinner for only our families. It was the first time since our youth, that my brother and I had hunted deer all week and then spent Thanksgiving together with everyone at the table having the same last name.

Old recipes like Grandma Ellis' green beans and oyster dressing were shared with the next generation of Ellis'. My brother and I recalled the Thanksgivings of our youth through food and hunting stories while our children and wives rolled their eyes at us and laughed. For a brief moment in time, I was a kid again.

I absolutely love Thanksgiving. For people who treasure hunting and sharing nature's bounty, it is an awesome time of year.

Maybe I am just getting older and more sentimental about Thanksgiving and want to hold on to the week a little longer each year. Don't get me wrong; I adore Christmas. But I think I'll let November belong to Thanksgiving as long as I can.

TRUCKS

School has started. Starlings are beginning to flock together in huge black bands that flow like a river across the sky. Football is back and of course, Mountaineer fans are hopeful. For outdoor folks, camouflage is the attire of choice and archery targets decorate our lawns. All are signs that fall is near, but the true indicator to most sportsmen is the condition of their trucks.

Our trucks transform from a vehicle that hauls passengers into a hunting rig. Like all natural phases the transformation occurs in stages. The first phase, lets simply call it the larva stage, is when washing the truck is no longer routine. Traveling down mud roads scouting for bucks and hanging stands does not lend itself to a clean truck. My truck will not see a wash bucket until well into spring. Several scratches and dings occur during this stage and it should be noted that blemishes are just part of the juvenile process.

The second phase, let's call it the pupa stage, is when the floor board is littered with various debris that is also covered in the remainders of the larva phase, mud. Debris can range from empty bottles of water, snack cake wrappers, spent cartridges, fast food bags, a few worn out posted signs, and of course your bow. A bow should never be taken out of the hunting rig. Every hunter knows that the proper way to store your hunting equipment is in the passenger side seat.

It is during this phase that the truck bed becomes a very useful tool. There should be visible evidence of stand hanging, deer feeding, and food plot preparation. A good length of rope or chain should be strewn as well as several models of tree pegs and ratchet straps. An ATV is allowed to remain parked in the bed during this phase. It is not visible on all rigs, but very common in West Virginia.

The third phase, let's call it the winged adult, is when the hunting rig hits maturity. The color of the sides will be a faded mud brown with every available inch of cab space used for the storage of hunting related materials. The inside of the truck should resemble the bargain bin at a Cabela store. At a minimum, three sets of camouflage clothing and a good set of raingear will be present. Somewhere stuffed in the seats or console should be four flashlights, two without batteries and a half roll of toilet paper. The dash should have two knives, binoculars, an extra hat and a half empty pack of broadheads. The smell inside the cab should resemble a mixture of french fries and buck lure.

There is no more exciting time for the hunter than the eve of fall. I hope to see you on the back roads, you can't miss me, and I'll be the one in the hunting rig.

ABOVE ALL, HE WAS A FISHERMAN

Fishing surrounds my earliest memories of my grandfather. He loved to wade in clear creeks and he took pride in his fishing tackle. He was also a father, a foreman at a local plant, member of the church, a Mason, a gardener, and a fine wood worker. But to me, he was a fisherman.

When the stresses of life, family, and work begin to draw in on me I escape to the only place that I can find "calm." The process begins the evening before I fish. I watch the weather, predict the levels of the creek, and choose a handful of fly patterns. The old patterns of flies are like old friends, dependable and predictable. Fishing to me is not so much about catching fish; it is about a form of therapy that allows me to recharge.

Upon arrival, the ritual is always the same. The tailgate serves as a bench to sit and watch the creek as I put on waders and rig my fly rod. The sound of the creek and the smell of rushing waters are the first stages of therapy. The first step in the creek is always the same. I look at my rod to make sure it is seated straight, I feel the water to gauge its temperature, and I scan the first run to see where a trout might live. The first few casts are usually awkward due to rusty shoulders.

As I walk up the creek dialing my casts in and

actually begin fishing, time escapes me. The world begins to shrink and my senses become acute. I am simply fishing and my mind and body move slowly.

Sometime during this transformation, my casts begin to work and I start catching fish. The first fish of the day is magic. I take my time landing the fish carefully and pause before releasing it. During this pause, Grandad comes to mind as if he was fishing right beside me. I hold the trout up out of habit, so that he can see my catch. As I slip the trout nose first into the current, I am healed. Sitting on a rock in the middle of a cold stream, I begin to feel "calm."

The fishing trip ends, not based on time, but when I am mentally healed and the tell tale signs of fatigue set in. It usually comes with a faulty cast into a tree, or I notice that I have to straighten out my back. On the trip home I drive a little slower, the windows are almost always down, and I am new. The waders will be hung on the coat rack, the vest hung on its hook, and the fly rod stored against the living room wall.

Thanks Grandad for taking me fishing again, I will sleep well.

FARM POND

It all started with an invitation. Although I am no spring chicken, peer pressure still exists. I just couldn't resist. I had to take him up on his offer.

It was a low-key afternoon with not much going on, when a friend stopped by the office to chat. This friend happens to be a professional fishing guide and I always enjoy hearing "tales from the guide's seat." I love fishing stories. I don't even particularly care if they are made up, ones that grow quickly like garden tomatoes freshly watered with Miracle-Gro, as long as they are told correctly. Give me a passionate lie about the number of fish or the size of the one that you lost at the boat and I am a happy camper.

In the middle of our conversation, he dropped the bomb. "If you need a place to fish after work someday, you are more than welcome to fish in my farm pond." That precise moment is when my troubles began.

To many, a farm pond is simply a ditch or hole in a hayfield. To me, they are one of West Virginia's best-kept secrets. Why you may ask? Because we are blessed with so much water to fish that the old cattail-lined, murky pond often gets overlooked. When I see a farm pond I think of fish growing uninterrupted by humans, waiting for some worn out fisherman to throw them a night crawler on a rusty hook. I think of huge fish and the heart of my problem, new state records. There I said it! According to my therapists, step one is admitting your problem.

When I get an invitation to fish a pond from a farmer who states, "There used to be some big fish in there. Not sure now, haven't fished it for years," I can't help myself. I have to go find out what lies beneath the lily pads.

To prove that I am not nuts, well not totally, I have proof that our state's watering holes have provided more than one angler with a fish of a lifetime. If you happen to flip to the state records section of the DNR Fishing Regulations, you will see my point. Species like largemouth bass, rainbow trout, yellow perch, bluegill, carp and bowfin all have one thing in common. They were all caught in ponds!

This summer, I have dedicated a good deal of my fishing time to ponds. I have not caught any record fish yet, but I have caught some real lunkers. If you happen to see me driving down some dirt road with a topo map spread across the dash of my truck, fishing rods dangling out of the bed and a crazed look in my eyes don't mind me. I will get over this phase soon enough.

That is, soon enough I hope for squirrel season. I heard through the grapevine that Old Man Landis had some huge fox squirrels living on his farm. I should probably stop and see him before too long. I wonder if he has a farm pond? Yep, this is generally how it starts.

CARP, ROUND 2

This story is about my multiple failed attempts at catching a carp. It began with a little couch time and a TV. People have been warning our society of the ill effects of the combination for years. I should have listened closer. During an episode of *River Monsters*, a show where host Jeremy Wade uncovers the world's largest, strangest and most dangerous fish, the idea hit me. I want to go catch something big right here at home.

My goal was to catch a monster carp within my home county. How big does a carp have to be to be considered a monster? The state records are roughly 40 inches long and over 40 pounds. Why not go big if you are going to go at all. (Optimism is a dandy thing, especially when sitting on your couch) After all, I remember catching bunches of carp as a kid with worn out equipment and a rusty hook.

I failed the challenge miserably. In fact, the challenge changed from trying to catch a monster carp to trying to catch any carp. I fished hard. I had sound advice from the DNR and several letters from readers to guide me. In fact, I had an amazing call from a local angler giving me directions to his "honey-hole." Nonetheless, man versed fish and the fish won.

The challenge haunted me like a bad dream. This summer I once again started researching baits, rigs and studying carp behavior and diet. I decided it was time to break the curse or forever be known as the man who couldn't catch a carp. I refused to give in. The stakes were simply too high.

With a weekend set aside for fishing and with water levels and weather pristine, I resumed the challenge and jumped headfirst into the madness. We set course for the swirly waters of the famed New River.

Day one was no real surprise; no carp partially because the urge to bass fish took over my primal instincts. Day two was a little better; I managed to fish for carp in the morning but gave way again to the urge to cast for bass in the early afternoon. I was slipping off the carp challenge and I needed to regroup.

The evening fishing plans were drawn and only carp rigs and baits were allowed. We headed to a yet another carp destination. With the sun sinking, in the shadows along the banks of the river and with witnesses present and willing to verify species and length, a carp was caught. In fact, more than one was caught. The curse of the carp was lifted and an angler returned home victorious.

Next challenge? Monster muskies—stay tuned, this might take awhile.

DAD'S DAY

I am often asked how to get a job in the outdoor industry. There is no real answer besides raw determination sprinkled with a whole bunch of luck. For those who are interested, I ran across this job posting the other day.

Wanted:

A self-motivated person who is knowledgeable in the arts of outdoor pursuits, who possesses a willingness to share experiences and enjoys watching others be successful.

Qualifications required but not limited to:

Applicant must be able to set alarm for unthinkable wakeup times, drive in any weather condition, skin deer, fry fish, scout deer stands, feed dogs, untangle knotted fishing lines, sharpen knives, hang tree stands, whittle sticks, build fires even when it is raining, pitch tents, cut firewood, tell direction by the moon, row rivers, start outboard motors, load ATVs, run trot lines, butcher game, fillet fish, run fast, shoot straight, track deer, paddle a canoe, climb a tree, gig frogs, seine minnows, cast a fly rod, turn over rocks for worms, pack lunches, change batteries in small flashlights, carry heavy packs, drag deer over steep hills, climb mountains, use a compass, read maps, sleep in trucks and stinky campers, carry a handkerchief, pack extra socks, carry water, call in turkeys, build hunting blinds, catch fish of any species, pack in a week's worth of groceries, tie a knot, re-spool a bait casting reel, predict the weather, tune a bow, load a muzzleloader, catch night crawlers, throw a cast net, surf fish, tie flies, reload ammunition, tell direction by the sun, identify the constellations, know when the rut occurs, get trucks unstuck from mud holes, make bologna sandwich on a dash board, administer basic first aid, call in coyotes, make jerky, skip rocks, swim, tell campfire stories, hoot like an owl, carry extra toilet paper, sit still, laugh at bad jokes, tie shoes multiple times a day, remember the snacks, pack out a bear, know every bird by song, have adequate knowledge of the "good ole days", land fish with a net, make carp bait out of bread, chum fish, string a bow, hit a target out of the air with a shotgun, cut kindling, pluck a goose, cross fallen logs, find lost dogs, doctor the ill, cut bait, make a meal out of Vienna Sausages, get fish hooks out of body parts, ask permission from landowners to hunt, book trips to far away places, light a Coleman lantern, cook over a fire, pack a cooler, load the truck, remember the hand warmers, go to bed late, fry bacon, troll for trout, skin squirrels, chase rabbits, make a forked stick

into a rod holder, tell time, throw a buzz bait,
predict deer movement, pull arrows from targets,
know port from starboard, identify snakes,
untangle fishing lures, be patient, loving, kind and
make adventures that create memories that last a
lifetime.
   Pay Scale:
   No monetary rewards offered.
   Benefits:
   Being a dad.

Thank you to all the fathers out there who take the time to share their time with others afield.

GRANDAD'S CATALOG

A few days ago, while searching for a book to accompany me across the country and to help to curb the boredom of airports, I stumbled across the *Bass Pro Shops Master Catalog* on my shelf.

I flipped through the pages of the massive catalog and it felt oddly familiar. I have received the catalog as long as I can remember and have dog-eared its pages many, many times. But this feeling was more than just shopping through a catalog—it was much deeper than that. Perhaps it was the quiet of the evening or the glimpse of snow falling through the window or maybe both that caused a flood of memories on a cold, dark winter's night.

In those memories, I was a child sitting in my Grandfather's living room next to the fireplace. He was sitting beside me. I was flipping the pages as he described how to use the lures and what fish they were intended for. Often the lure on the page would trigger a story of a fish—a Rapala double-jointed minnow and a smallmouth bass that hit the bait in the haze of a humid summer morning or a Rooster Tail spinner and a hole full of trout on a steep mountain creek.

The big baits intrigued me and Grandfather's description of the walleyes and northern pike he had caught on his many trips to Canada kept me spellbound. I could see through his words the lure in the dark waters and the strike of a monster pike causing the water to explode. He took me with him on many fishing adventures by means of his stories and the pictures on the pages of the catalog.

After the last page was flipped, we often would head into the basement to look at his fishing gear. He had a big plastic box with slide-out drawers that served as storage device for his tackle. Each drawer was labeled by the species the lures inside were intended for. Once the drawer was slid out, I could see the lures—many of which I saw on the catalog's pages and heard about in his fishing tales. As a child, the magic of holding in your hands the lure that your hero used to catch the big fish in his stories was unforgettable.

As the winter's winds rattled the loose screen in the den, I was startled back to my task at hand of finding a good book for an upcoming trip. I closed the catalog and placed it neatly back on the shelves with the other books. I miss my grandfather daily but I can still hear his words in the pages of a fishing tackle catalog and smile when a tie on one of his favorite lures and fool a fish into a strike. I know he does too.

FISHING TALE

It was time to fish. The songbirds greet every morning with a zest of a new beautiful day being born. Male turkeys announce their joy for spring by gobbling at everything including themselves. The grass is awakening from winter dormancy, spring flowers are in bloom and the mountains are transitioning from grays to shades of green.

The only problem with my longing for tight lines and cold, gin clear waters was one simple fact. My normal and cherished fishing waters were big and running high. They were less than ideal to say the least. But, the urge for fresh air and the West Virginia spring ritual of trout fishing was not going to be denied by the weather.

A quick look at the weather indicated a fast approaching cold front with more rain. My options were all leaning towards lake or pond fishing. Fishing for trout in lakes is generally not my plan a, b, or c but again, my options were limited with the high creeks and pending afternoon storms.

It has been a while since I have bank fished for trout. I generally prefer wading or at least fishing moving waters. With lines set and the cork handles of the rods resting patiently in rod holders, we sat in our camp chairs and waited. The first hour marched by. Out of boredom or thinking maybe our initial casts were off their mark, we reeled in our lines and baited the hooks with fresh bait. Into the next half hour, we waited with no action.

As the skies darkened and the wind began to pick up, causing the surface of the lake to become choppy, the stock trout switch was flipped. The next hour of fishing was a full blown, first-rate fishing bonanza.

I have heard since I was a child the tale of fish gorging themselves right before a big storm.

Having fished my entire life and even spent a few years guiding people to fish, my judgment on the right-before-a-storm tale is filed under the "not certain" category.

But this time was different and now I'll be the one spreading the wisdom of fish biting right before a storm to all who ask me, "How's the fishing been?" I will grin and gladly tell my fishing story and who knows, maybe I'll even begin to believe the fishing tale.

MUSKY

There is an antique fish mount on the wall of my office.
The fish is a musky that was caught in West Virginia
on January 9, 1972. The musky was given to me as a
gift. I have had a connection to muskies for as long as
I can remember. And for some time now, the month of
January reminds me of that fish and of how strong my
connection to the species is.

Growing up on the banks of the Elk River in the
70s, fishing was the talk of the small town where we
lived. And the news of someone catching a large musky
spread across the town quicker than gossip and caused
us to rush to see the giant fish and proud angler.

It seemed to me back then, everyone in town fished.
Most of us were smallmouth fisherman, who enjoyed
floating the river in a canoe or wading the river casting
baits in the shoals of the summertime months. Others
fished at night and could be seen in the glow of their
lanterns on the banks of the river's deep pools.

But the most interesting people to me in those days,
were the ones who fished when the water ran cold and
slow and who talked of monsters. They took on the
sport of fishing like hunters in search of the mystical
trophy buck that was very rarely seen and was talked
about like a ghost.

I have had many musky encounters on the rivers of my fishing career. I have even managed to net a few. But the big musky, the one on file from my mind from childhood, has eluded me. I have seen him swirl at my bait, even had him on my hook for a brief moment, but I have never held him in my hands.

So as another January rolls on by and I am reminded of the fish that hangs on my wall, I catch myself daydreaming of a future day when I finally touch the musky of my childhood dreams. I am hopeful this is the year.

SMILING LIKE A KID

Growing up on the banks of the Elk River, I believed that summertime was carved out of the calendar so that people could fish. Fishing used to be getting good right about the last days of school when the air temperatures began to warm. I have colorful memories of looking out the window of the classroom at an eddy in the rivers current. Looking at the swirly waters, thoughts of smallmouth bass chasing schools of minnows would race through my mind.

Thinking back on the fishing of my youth, things were much simpler. I had a rod and reel. I had a plastic box with a makeshift collection of hooks, bobbers and sinkers. Upon inspection, you may find a lure I was given by an adult for my birthday but most often I lost it, and replaced it with one or two musky lures I found stuck in a log or tree along the river. I had the basics and that is all I needed to fish for the summer—hook tied on to string.

The one thing I learned early on in my fishing was the importance of bait. Bait determined it all. My neighbor's backyard when freshly mowed on a humid summer night meant night crawlers. All I needed was a flashlight that had fresh enough batteries to last until the coffee can was full.

Night crawlers meant blue gills and crappie along the brushy waters of the bank. They meant when allowed, staying up late to catch catfish in the slow pools of the river. The adults would talk of prized bait like spring lizards, crawdads and minnows. So we learned to catch them by stomping creeks, setting traps and seining pockets of the river.

A pile of prized bait often meant an invitation to float the river or wade the big shoals where the trophy smallmouth live. There was no prouder moment as a kid to hand an adult bait from a bucket full of your hard work and efforts. And when that bait brought the strike of a smallmouth and a hook set from the adult, the connection you felt to the process of fishing using the food chain and the natural world was strong and powerful.

On a river float trip this past week fishing for smallmouth bass, I found myself smiling at a simple memory from my childhood. I was smiling and acting like a kid; just like the boy that was fishing with me.

WILD BROWN TROUT

As sportsmen, we all have a bucket list of adventures we would love to take part in. For some, an African safari and miles of openness sounds alluring while some dream of the Rocky Mountains. Wherever it is—it is fun to daydream about the pursuit of animals in far off places.

Having said that, maybe your dream of hunting far from home includes somewhere in West Virginia. Perhaps giant white-tailed deer in our southern counties, black bears in our mountains or maybe turkeys up north—our state does have a lot to offer. We all would likely admit, we are spoiled with hunting and fishing here at home.

I have had two days hunting and fishing in West Virginia I would consider to be "bucket list" worthy. I recall a few turkey hunts and squirrel hunts that would qualify.

There have been days on the Elk, the New, the South Branch as well as miles of wild trout streams that were very special to me and would rank up there with the best in the country. Our smallmouth streams and trout waters are top shelf.

But there is something about floating the Yellowstone River, fishing offshore in the Gulf of Mexico for tuna, New England for stripers, Canada for northern pike and walleyes that makes us want to pack our bags and book a plane ticket. Maybe it's simply the thought of going somewhere new and adventurous that moves our souls.

My career has taken me all over and I have heard all kinds of tales of "we have the best hunting and fishing" in the world. While much of it is simply marketing hype, there have been a few times I was pleasantly surprised.

Some of my surprises were elk hunting in New Mexico, turkey hunting in Oklahoma, fishing for redfish in Louisiana and tuna fishing in Venice.

A few weeks ago, a group of us traveled to Mexico's Lake El Salto for four days of fishing. Lake El Salto is well known, it is not like we found a hidden gem, but the fishing simply blew away any expectations I left home with. Growing up fishing rivers, I am not much of a largemouth bass fisherman. Having said that, Lake El Salto may have changed that. The fish were unbelievably big, hit the baits very hard and were very powerful fighters and most memorable, very plentiful.

My next adventure on my list you may ask? An undisclosed location in my home county for wild brown trout. With the heat and humidity, the bugs are flying around like crazy and the fish are gorging themselves and becoming fat—I don't plan on missing this time of year at home.

HOME, SWEET HOME

Returning from the world's largest sport fishing trade show in Orlando, I came home ready to fish! After four days of walking the convention center filled with the gear, apparel and accessories that help to make a day on the water both exciting and rewarding, I was ready to set the hook.

If the gear wasn't enough to get your fishing mood in pure excitement mode, running into and having conversations with some of the best anglers in the world will certainly seal the deal. After looking at whopper fish pictures, listening to stories of world-class fishing and seeing all the latest and greatest gear, I was ready to get home to fish.

With bags still packed, and after a much needed all night nap, I executed the plan I had been working on since I left Orlando. With the weather man saying simply, "It's another hot one today" I loaded my truck for a trip to the coldest creek I could think of.

I parked under a huge white oak tree next to the creek hoping the shade would keep the inside of my truck from turning into an Easy Bake Oven and crunched my way in wading shoes to the creek's edge. There are few great feelings and memories a hot summer day in July can provide and one of those is stepping in a mountain creek—the cool water rushing into your wading shoes gives you a quick shock of the chills.

After five days in Orlando, I was finding it hard to slow down my pace. My casts were hurried. I wasn't happy with my knot; I tied the fly on with haste. I was racing up the creek stomping my feet. I learned all this the hard way when I spooked a trout feeding in a little run. The fish darted up the creek like a bear was after it. I needed to slow down.

Finally, I convinced myself that this evening of fishing was not a race. There were no planes to catch and no crowds of people to see. It was just me and the babble of clear, cold creek.

As I approached a deep hole filled with shadows and moss-covered rocks along its banks, I could feel the temperature change in the air immediately. I was in secret pocket of the world and it looked fishy. I sat down and retied my fly. I took a deep breath and filled my lungs with clean mountain air. I presented the fly upstream and made a quick downstream mend in my line. The fly was drifting perfectly down a seam of the creek. Somewhere from deep in the hole of water, a trout rose slowly to look at my fly. After a long inspection, the trout opened its mouth and slurped in the fly. The take was just a sip. I raised my rod tip and made the connection. It felt great to be home again.

A DAY WITH HEMINGWAY

As an outdoor columnist, I find it my responsibility to find topics that are relevant to my audience. With our seasons offering such an abundance of wildlife and wild places to pursue our passions, it is with pleasure that I write 500-700 words on the topic of the outdoor arts of home. Throw in a deer season, turkey season, trout fishing, smallmouth bass and a few other species and seasons, and well, I am on roll. To put it frankly—I love my job of putting words on paper.

This week, however, I broke my normal routine. The start of my story begins with me having a conversation about a bucket list of species of fish with a friend. Being from Arizona, he was not overly familiar with fishing and its species of game fish, but when I asked him if he would like to join me in the pursuit of a famed Marlin in the saltwater fishing community, his face lit up.

"You mean the fish in *The Old Man and the Sea*," he asked.

"Exactly," I replied.

Remembering Hemingway's classic novel and the fish being such a huge part of the story. A day on the blue waters with a chance, albeit very small, a chance nonetheless of matching wits with what many consider the greatest game fish in the world sounded wonderful.

I booked a day of offshore fishing with a fulltime offshore captain. When I stated we wanted to concentrate on blue marlin, he responded in a very low voice, "They are around in these waters—come on out and let's see if we can find a hungry one."

The morning came and we found ourselves riding to the fishing grounds with pure excitement. But after many hours of trolling the lack of action and length of time was not on our side. It was simply a boat ride in a very beautiful place in this world.

Not to spoil the rest of the article, but there was a fish involved in this story—a great big fish in fact. The truth of the matter is, we caught and released a blue marlin and in doing so, a new fisherman will become a lifelong person who fishes and a lifelong fisherman crossed off a species on his bucket list. Maybe not a day worthy of a Hemingway story, but indeed a great day on the blue water.

CALM BEFORE THE STORM

The loud dinging sound from the phone startled me. The noise was prompted from a weather app notifying me of a thunderstorm approaching. "Great," I thought. "There goes my evening fishing plan."

After work, I checked radar and the ding was correct; a line of heavy thunderstorms was making a beeline for our area. "I'm going anyhow," I mumbled. "To heck with it."

I made it to the creek as the skies began to darken. I hurriedly slid on my wading boots and crawled over the bank to the creek's edge. The water was ideal. In the run before me, I identified three hiding spots I thought a trout might be holding. It was in the third run, after a poor cast and line mend, a trout lunged at the fly and startled me into setting the hook into nothing but air. "Slow down," I said to myself in a gruff voice. I was in a hurry to beat the storm.

In a tricky little spot under a fallen tree, a trout moved to my dropper fly but did not eat it. After three more attempts, the trout stuck his nose towards the dry fly but again did not eat it. "I don't have time for a finicky trout," I thought.

In a run I have fished for many years, I stopped to sit on a rock and as the wind swirled, I could feel the temperature drop and could smell fresh rain. It was raining hard somewhere upstream as the creek appeared to carrying more water and I noticed a few leaves making their way swiftly down the current.

I checked my tandem-fly rig, straightened my leader and began the progression of casting my line further and further into the run. When I had enough distance in my cast, I dropped my rod tip allowing the fly to drop quietly onto the surface. I quickly mended my slack line and stripped in the fly line back to me as the fly drifted downstream towards my feet.

Midway through the drift, a trout smacked the dropper fly hard and began to run upstream away from me, causing all the slack line to go with it. I raised my rod tip and the trout responded by digging deeper into the current. A big clap of thunder slowly rolled down the valley as I dipped my net into the current to retrieve the fish. A stocky brown trout greeted me and I quickly slid him headfirst back into the water.

Safely back at the truck, I watched as the skies opened up and let loose a major thunderstorm with hail, lightning, winds and buckets of rain. It was there that I gave thanks for the opportunity to go fishing and enough time before the storm hit to lay hands on a fine brown trout. It was a good day.

ELLIS BROTHERS OPENING DAY

This spring will be my 29th season of spring gobbler hunting. It's simply hard for me to believe and I am the one who was there for each and every season. The reason I am certain of the number is that I was asked by someone lately and I had to stop and think about it.

The reason for the inquiry is the production of a film series on turkey hunting and an invitation to join a group of friends in south Florida to hunt turkeys. The production team needed some old guys to interview about their obsession. You guessed it—I'm one of the old guys.

The question, "How long have you been turkey hunting," seemed odd to my ears and it caught me off guard. It was something I hadn't ever thought about. I am aware that my brother and I started hunting turkeys when I was in high school, but that doesn't seem like that long ago.

My brother and I were walleye fishing the other day and with this question on my mind, I asked him to verify my memory on my turkey hunting past since he is older than me by four years.

Here is how it happened in my mind—the way I became a turkey hunter. My brother was asked to join a group of hunters who set up their annual fall camp in the Mon National Forest. Since my brother and I were accomplished bow-hunters, he accepted the invitation and prepared himself to go bow-hunting for whitetails.

But there were other hunters in camp and some of them were fall turkey hunters. Being musically inclined, my brother became interested in the calls they used to mimic the sounds of hen turkeys. He was hooked.

He was fascinated with the calls and began to practice with a mouth call until he became, well, very good at it. Because music had been a big part of his life, he could hear the pitch, the cadence and the sounds of the wild turkey in his head and learned quickly to make those sounds with his calls.

I recall the very first adult gobbler that ever came to our calls and I can still see the excitement on my brother's face as he carried the bird off that steep hillside farm. In fact, I don't have to think very hard for a flood of memories of turkeys over the years that have come in to our calls.

I hunt with my brother every opening day of the West Virginia spring gobbler season to this day and I plan on doing so until the bell rings for me to come home. I plan on making it at least another 29 seasons.

NOT THE BEST FISHING DAY EVER

In the midst of my grind of chores, work-related projects and life in general—Mother Nature threw me a bone. Somehow, I found myself in a full-blown, hard-as-you-can-go rut. Between grass cutting, work, household chores, more work, family responsibilities, honey-do's and scheduled maintenance, I was running fast and not getting anywhere. I was in a midsummer doldrum and in need of a breather.

And then as if scripted, the weather shifted from hot and muggy to a slight cool down that blanketed southern West Virginia. A small front blew through with a few rainstorms and showers leaving behind a crisp, clear, bright day. If you tried hard enough and squinted your eyes just right, you could feel and taste a hint of fall in the air. Albeit very small, I took the sign— hook, line and sinker.

I needed to wash the summertime work off my soul. I was longing for cool waters, shade and the sounds and smell only a fast-moving creek or river can provide. It was time to fish.

Knowing that my schedule couldn't hold much more weight without collapsing; I rolled the dice and threw caution to the wind. Adding a day of fishing was risky and I knew that something was going to have to wait on my return, but it was a gamble I was willing to take.

My plan was simple—fly rod, flies, cooler lunch and no watch. Somehow not wearing a watch would slow down time, at least, that was my thought. With gear packed and with a light heart, I rolled down the windows of the truck and headed to my go-to creek.

As I rounded the curve, I got my first look at the water. It is part of my ritual every time I fish it. I pull over at the wide spot when the creek is first visible, look at the water and say out loud to whoever is with me in the truck or alone, the condition of the creek.

"Stained and running a tad high, but fishable," I said aloud to myself.

The recent rains had the creek running high and its waters cloudy—almost ideal conditions to fool a summertime trout into striking my fly.

I parked just off the road adjacent to the best runs in the creek. This was not the time for scouting new sections or playing around with new fly patters—my plan called for a straightforward approach to maximize my allotted time on the creek.

My casts were hurried and sloppy, the fish were not exceptionally active and the day did not play out as the "best day of fishing ever." But none of that mattered. What mattered was I marked a day on my calendar as a Fishing Day and that is exactly what I did—I went fishing. It was glorious.

MULE DEER HUNT

It was a long night and I was simply too tired to sleep. I spent the restless night listening to the winter wind howl and from the light of the cabin I could see it was still snowing. It was going to be another long day and I was already exhausted. I was missing my West Virginia home severely.

When the alarm from my cell phone chirped, I wasn't sure if I could move. I slowly lifted my legs and swung my feet towards the floor. Momentum carried the rest of my body until I was standing. "I can do this one more day," I told myself. It was day five of a weeklong hunt and the subzero temperatures, the altitude and physically demanding terrain had my body and mind questioning the sanity of the hunt.

Each day of the hunt started the same. We would gather at the base with the use of high magnification optics, we would scan the terrain for mountain mule deer high in the Colorado Rockies.

The plan was to be there when the weather was bitter cold and the animals would be on the move. The mating season was in full swing making the mule deer even more unpredictable. Once we spotted a mature deer, most often times many miles away, we would devise a plan on how we would move humans to a location close enough to actually begin to hunt him.

The problem with high altitude is the ability to breathe. The first days in high altitude causes intense headaches and fatigue. It is like trying to hike with the flu. Add in the bitter cold and uphill walking and your body can only handle so much no matter how good a shape you are in.

By the fifth day, I came to the realization that I had enough energy for one good stalk per day. The stalk would start with minimal clothing and as we gained elevation, I would add clothing to fight the cold, trying not to get overheated and sweat.

I would rest often and drink water every chance I would get to fend off dehydration headaches. Many stalks that week ended with long periods of sitting and waiting for the deer we saw that morning to show up. Most often times the deer had other plans as I watched brilliant sunsets, bundled up shivering, wondering how in the world I was going to get off the mountain by dawn.

This particular morning, we spotted a herd of deer with a mature buck following close behind them. They were high on the mountain but moving fast downhill at an angle that might just give us a chance. We hurriedly stuffed our backpacks full of enough gear to withstand the elements for the stalk. Moving slowly as to not break a sweat in the single digit temperatures, we hiked uphill.

As we topped the rise, overlooking a long and narrow sagebrush valley, there he was. My chest heaved as my lungs filled themselves with ice-cold mountain air trying to extract the oxygen my body craved. I watched the mature buck move slowly across the valley. I took my backpack off and laid it in the snow for a steady rest for my rifle. With me laying flat on the ground, the crosshairs in the scope moved with my breathing and I had no choice but to wait for my lungs and heart rate to slow. He continued walking away. I closed my eyes to calm my nerves. What felt like an eternity later, I opened my eyes and the crosshairs aligned and the trigger broke precisely on the mark. My hunt was over.

Hunting mountain mule deer was one of the most challenging adventures I have ever experienced. For me, hunting is a freedom that inspires passion and a spiritual connection to the natural world. It was a fine day and I was glad to be part of it.

KEYS TO THE GATE

Big bucks with massive antlers are a young hunter's dream. Every magazine has a section dedicated to "tried and true" tips on how to become a better hunter. An evening spent watching outdoor programming will lend a hunter to believe that it can't be that hard to take a trophy deer because three were just taken in a 30-minute show.

In reality land, which is where most all hillbillies live, it just isn't so. Most of us will hunt our entire life for a rare chance to encounter a trophy.

When I first started working in the outdoor industry, I had a chance encounter with a Hall of Fame bowhunter. We were at a restaurant waiting for the rest of our party to show up. With time on our hands, I decided to pick his brain about bowhunting. Being nervous and young, my questions were not hitting the mark so I bluntly asked, "What is the one secret, I mean, suggestion you would give bowhunters who are looking to become trophy hunters?"

He paused a second or two while my mind was racing to predict his answer. Would his answer be tree stand placement, human scent elimination, tracking, hunting the rut; the silence was too much for my mind to handle. As I tried not to fidget like my son in church, he responded, "Keys to the gate."

I thanked him for his time and quickly retreated to the restroom in search of some clarity. I splashed some water on my face and returned to the table hoping the rest of party had arrived and there were no seats left for me.

When I returned, the bowhunter made me feel at ease. What took place next was one of the most enjoyable conversations I have ever had. He explained his statement by telling me that bowhunting is not about trophies. It is simply about being in tune with nature and getting close to the animals.

Yes, he has shot numerous record book animals but not because he is a superior hunter or more gifted than most with a stick and string. In fact, he told me that he is no better hunter than most; he was simply afforded the opportunity throughout his career to be invited to hunt where trophy animals live.

That evening in the hotel room it hit me. He was right. Celebrity hunters are not necessarily better hunters; they simply have "keys to the gate."

POP'S GARDEN

With many of us planting our gardens, I am reminded of the best gardener and storyteller I have ever known. My grandfather had a garden out in the country. It required an exciting car trip for a young boy, over curvy gravel roads, past freshly cut hayfields. The smells, sounds and sights that flooded the car through rolled-down windows provided a feeling of freedom for me.

Once we arrived at his garden, I was set free to run and chase grasshoppers or frogs down near the pond while he got his chores done in the tidy little rows of tilled earth. Occasionally, he would look up and whistle and like a groundhog, I would lift my head high in the field and wave my hand so he could see me and would know I was okay.

When I got tired of running, I would make my way back to the garden and plop down under a shade tree next to the creek. He would walk over and sit a spell with me and ask if I wanted to help. I always wanted to help him.

He would set me in a certain area of the garden and I would pull weeds or chuck rocks until he returned to inspect my work. We would then walk the rows of plants while he told me about each one and their particulars—this plant likes acid soil, this one needs plenty of room to run, these needs stakes to hold them up and so on. This part of the garden trip always bored me and he knew it.

After my lesson, he would release me to the shallow creek were I could cool off and build pools to hold caught minnows and crawdads.

If it was late enough in the summer for ripe vegetables to be picked, he would place them in a basket in the backseat of his car. On the way home, he would stop by a few places and leave the vegetables on the porch or hand deliver to older folks as they smiled and thanked him. I recall many times returning home with an empty basket and I could never understand why he worked so hard in the hot sun to raise vegetables only to give most of them away.

My grandfather was not a teacher by trade. He was not a master gardener. But he was a man who understood the value of sharing a time-honored skill of raising a garden and a grandson. He also understood the importance of sharing with others in need.

I can't recall a summer of my youth that didn't include days walking the rows of tilled earth with him. And I remember his lessons daily as I walk through the rows of my life.

THE OLD SIDE BY SIDE

Well it happened. I was told it was going to but I never believed them. In fact, I fought the notion and was very adamant it wasn't going to sneak up on me and grab me while I wasn't paying attention. It did. I am getting old.

My friend once told me long ago that an object could trigger a happy memory of long ago and I would want that object to remind me of the happiness. Now before you spit your coffee back into your cup and proclaim your local outdoor writer has lost his marbles, hear me out. It's simple really.

It happened to me and came out of left field. It was an old double barrel shotgun, and not a particularly good one, but it was for sale. The old gun brought back a flood of memories when mostly older men would speak of woods full of grouse and old farms and briery fencerows full of rabbits. The speak and their words often contained talk of great hunting dogs, leather boots and of course double-barreled shotguns. And there was laughter and joy about their passion, their sport.

The old, tired side-by-side shotgun reminded me of that laughter and passion when hunting was much more common and sometimes a much more social event. I bought the shotgun and plan to carry it this fall on several hunts. Not to be retro cool, although it is retro and cool, but to see if the connection to the past can be brought into this modern world and perhaps, just perhaps the feelings of my youth can energize my steps and fuel the passion in my soul for all things wild and being an active participant in the natural world.

I'm glad to have the old shotgun in my gun safe and I plan on making many new memories afield in the fall hunting seasons to come—at least I didn't find an old Jeep that needed restoring, that sounds expensive. Who knows, maybe that will be my next project.

BLUEGILL FISH

My son is going through a childhood phase. Jack loves talking about animals, especially the moose. Many times we have loaded up the pickup and headed to the farm on a grand moose hunt. We stalk through the woods and creek bottoms in search of the largest species in the deer family. To this date we have never seen any on the cliffs of the Gauley River, but the thrill of the chase has been exciting.

Lately, he and his sister have turned their animal fascination to fish. When dad returns from fly-fishing, the interrogation begins about what kind of trout I caught and what they look like. Originally the images stored on the computer were support for my fly-fishing articles, but lately they have become a valuable research tool for trout species identification.

At my neighbor's pond, the fish fascination came full circle. Jack and I headed out for a fishing day unparalleled in modern history. We stopped to gain permission from the neighbor and he decided to join us. We decided to try his brother's farm pond because a recent fishing report had been circulating about his kids catching several bass, catfish, and even a carp or two. I could see the wheels turning in my son's head about the thoughts of catching new fish and what they

75

would look like. I could just picture his little mind thinking what a catfish looked like and what the heck a carp was. The farmer said he saw one that looked like it must have weighed 20 pounds. My son's expression was a blank cold stare. Twenty pounds! That is as big as the sharks on Shark Week!

We rigged up his fishing rod and he cast it out into the deep waters of the pond. He was poised and ready to fight any giant fish brave enough to bite his hook. The anticipation was high as the little angler's bobber began to move. It bounced, wiggled, and finally went under. He set the hook like the pros on tour do, and began to reel in his prize. The fight was long, interrupted by entanglement in a cattail, but finally the fish was beached.

"What is it, Daddy?"

"It's a bluegill, son."

He held the fish up and admired it for long time. He smiled as I released it back into the water. I could see the calm come over him and could tell he was ready to head back to the comforts of his home to relay to his mother and sister about the new kind of fish he had caught. He was an angler. It was his turn to return home tired and ready to tell a great fishing story about a foreign fish in a far off place.

As he ran into the house his mother asked, "How was it?"

Chest out and eyes wide he proclaimed, "I caught a bluegill fish!"

GRANDAD'S VALENTINE

Tomorrow we celebrate Valentine's Day. The kids will be passing around cards at school and adults will give gifts and dinners to show their loved ones just how much they care. The smells of construction paper hearts, flowers and chocolate will fill the air and the color red will be everywhere.

This holiday marks an idle time for many sportsmen but as true optimists, we know that spring will be here next month with its warm days and green grass.

As I felt the cold and watched the snow blanket the landscape this week, I had plenty of indoor times to reflect on Saint Valentine. Although the truth behind the Valentine legends is murky, the stories all agree on a sympathetic, heroic, and, of course, romantic figure.

With the thoughts of love and warmer days ahead, many of which I hope to spend fishing, my mind drifted to the thoughts of my childhood saint—Grandad.

Grandad made electrical conduit as a career, but to me, he was a fisherman. Not only was he a fisherman, he was a smallmouth fisherman. Of course he did all the stuff grown men are supposed to do, like raise a family, be active in church, love his wife and be kind and generous, but to a wide-eyed boy, none of that mattered.

After his night shift at the plant, he would wade the creeks with his carbide light to catch soft-shell craws. When the old metal bait can was full, he would return home to pack the fishing gear for a day of fishing. My job was simply to ride along and listen to his stories and when he waded the creek to fish, I was to hold the bait bucket and hand him another crawdad when his hook returned empty.

He was the master at reading currents and always took the time to instruct me where he thought the smallmouth bass would be and how to drift the bait towards the fish. His old work pants and leather boots slid quietly through the water and I was in awe how he could walk upstream without making a splash.

One of my favorite stories he told was about his biggest smallmouth he ever caught. He'd recount about a deep hole in the creek that had a fallen tree in it—the tree's roots stuck up on the bank while its trunk and top was in the deep water.

The hole was too deep to wade and the slow current made the water's surface like glass and you could see every rock on the bottom and in turn, every fish could see you. Most fishermen would cast a time or two in the hole and then move on. But Grandad knew there would be an old, smart fish hiding under that log in the cool deep water.

He waited until a hot August day to belly crawl along the bank so as to not spook any fish. Once he reached the tree, he baited his hook—which was on the lightest line he had—with a soft-shell crawdad. (He didn't want to take any chances letting the fish see the line). He hooked the biggest crawdad in the bucket because he needed weight to get to the bottom but he knew if he used a sinker the splash when casting would spook the old lunker.

He tossed the crawdad under the log and fed slack into the line to let it sink naturally. The smallmouth took the crawdad and settled back to the bottom to rest. Grandad stood up, walked downstream to avoid any obstacles, winded in the slack line and set the hook. The greatest angler I have ever known had fooled the biggest bass in the creek.

This Valentine's day enjoy time with the ones you love. By simply writing these words, I spent time again with the person who showed me the true meaning of patience and love. Happy Valentine's Day Saint Grandad—thanks for taking me fishing.

FISHING TRIP
EIGHT YEARS IN THE MAKING

It was the warmest day yet this year. After a winter
that required us to enact a "shelter in place" for several
months, the sun's kind rays broke through the gray
winter day. The line at the Post Office was filled with
chatter about the warm weather and people were happy.
I was happy too because I was scheduled to take a client
fishing. It would be my first trip of the year.

This particular fishing outing had been in the
planning stages for more than 8 years. I had worked
out the details well in advance, but the timing and
execution had to be spot on to pull this one off. I have
known my fishing partner all his life and the promise
to take him fishing had come to fruition. With the
perfect weather conditions and snow run off waters still
running clear, it was the chance for him to catch his first
trout.

There is nothing simple about the first trip of the
season. My pickup time for the evening trip was to
occur at precisely 3:30 p.m. and I found myself spending
most of the day gathering gear, prepping the tackle and
hand packing a stream side dinner so we could spend all
the time we could together, fishing.

The ride to the river had a buzz to it; with raw
energy and excitement. I pulled the truck along side the

creek and we crawled over the bank to the water's edge. I pointed to the current and explained where I though the trout might be. His casts were rough at first; often missing the mark, but he overcame his inexperience and began to dial it in.

We fished the run hard to no avail and decided to try another spot. Each time we fished a new area the routine was the same. I would suggest where to cast, he would cast multiple times and no trout would respond. As the light began to fade, so did my hopes.

With the help of a sandwich and a can of pop, we decided to give it our all at one last riffle. The walk to the creek side was at a slower pace than the previous ones and by now he needed no more instruction.

He knew the drill and I watched as he cast upstream into the current. After several casts in the waning hours of a winter's evening, it happened! The trout took the bait and the novice angler worked the rod and reel. The rainbow trout was in hand and all his hard work and my years of planning boiled down to one perfect moment along a cold, clear, West Virginia creek.

That evening as I tucked the tired and proud angler into bed he asked, "Daddy, can we go fishing again sometime?"

THANKSGIVING DEER CAMP

For many of us, deer season pauses for Thanksgiving. Deer camps across the state sit idle while hunters travel back home to give thanks while eating too much turkey and dressing. For me, this year was different.

My son and I decided to spend the week afield hunting deer. The decision was made easier when travel plans of others were announced that did not include being home for the cherished meal. This year's Thanksgiving was going to be simply different and I planned on making it a great one.

Plans and lists were drawn and with hunting supplies procured, we set our sights to Jackson County. We stopped at the grocery store on the way out of town to fill our coolers with food for the seven-day outing. With the cart nearly overflowing with necessities like toilet paper and beef jerky, we headed to the big bin of frozen turkeys to purchase the needed menu items for our Thanksgiving dinner for two.

The turkey-day decorations mixed with the hustling people gathering their supplies for the annual feast, made me wonder if I was making the right decision of missing our family gathering. I was feeling a little gloomy and it must have showed on my face, when an acquaintance walked up and asked if I was okay.

"The Ellis boys are heading to deer camp for the week, missing our family's Thanksgiving and I am just trying to decide what we are going to eat," I said mumbling.

"What are you going to cook for you two?" she asked.

"I have no clue," I muttered.

"It's not hard, follow me," she said sternly snapping me out of my funk. "All you need is a small turkey breast, some stuffing and a can of gravy." As she quickly walked down the aisles, she pointed and told us what to put in our cart.

I thanked her for her help and wished her well. As we turned to walk away she said, "You know my son's most memorable Thanksgiving was the one he spent with his dad in deer camp. In fact, his Dad said it was his favorite too and he has had over 70 Thanksgivings."

She was right. The stuffing was mushy, the turkey was dry and rabbit ears on the TV didn't pick up the football game—we felt like the luckiest men on earth and gave thanks.

MISSED TURKEY

Several years ago, I hosted a writer on a turkey hunt here in West Virginia. The story line was simple; interview a famous turkey call manufacturer, take a tour of his facility and go hunt turkeys.

We had several days slotted for the hunt and I was confident in the location, the local knowledge and my new 3½ inch shotgun with its super tight choke that shot patterns that looked like a softball. All we needed was a bearded turkey to stand still long enough so that I could complete the task at hand.

Being young and confident looks great on a resume and often carries over well in a job interview but can be a real curse when hunting, especially turkeys. The location did indeed have plenty of turkeys. Most of them however decided they liked it better on the neighbor's property across the swollen creek.

Mid morning on the last day of our hunt, I got my chance. On a property we had permission to hunt, a gobbler let out a thunderous call in a small wood patch surrounded by a field. How was I going to walk across the field without spooking the turkey? A nearly impossible challenge with the "Duke Boys" tagging along so I rudely asked them to stay put.

I closed the distance to the wood line by low

crawling through the field. They found great pride in the fact that a turkey answered their raspy calls and it became very apparent that they were going to call to this turkey until he became hoarse from gobbling.

Each time they would call, I would cringe and the turkey would answer. I could tell he was right inside the woods strutting back and forth.

The turkey had grown tired of gobbling and began to walk in the open field right in the path of me. I first saw him about ten steps from me, and walking fast. When I could see his head clearly, I lifted the shotgun barrel and pulled the trigger. The gobbler made eye contact with me. I saw him laugh as he flew way without even ruffling a feather.

The walk back to my hunting party was not long enough for me to determine my excuse. The local turkey guides could not fathom how a grown man could miss a turkey at the end of his gun barrel and they had no trouble telling me that over and over. The only thing that slowed them down were bouts of uncontrollable belly laughter that made the truck swerve from ditch line to centerline as we drove back into town.

That was the last time I ever used a 3 ½-magnum turkey gun with a super full choke. I now pattern my shotgun at every distance from 15 to 40 yards and I am perfectly fine with a more open pattern.

I can still hear them laughing, especially the turkey.

I HUNT BECAUSE

I have been asked several times, especially after a long
week of chasing spring gobblers with nothing to show
for my efforts but exhaustion and embarrassment, why
I choose hunting as a leisure pursuit. The question used
to rattle me, to be honest. For a long time I was certain
why I hunted. But as a father, both will make one think
about things very differently, I have come to a place
in my life that I love to answer that question and take
pride in doing so.

My response, and one I care deeply about, is wildlife
conservation. In short, it is the hunters who pony-up
the funds for wildlife conservation. Since 1937, the
Pittman-Robertson Act establishes a federal funding
source for state wildlife conservation efforts. The money
does not come from a general tax fund, but it comes
directly from a self-imposed tax sportsmen asked to
be placed on the sale of most guns, ammo, bows and
arrows. The money then gets distributed back to the
states based on several factors including how many
paid hunting license holders the state has. In short,
if you love wildlife and want to help fund wildlife
management and restoration, buy a hunting license.

The system works well; just look at the number
bears, deer, turkey and other non-game animals

thriving today. Simply put, I hunt because I care about wildlife and wildlife managers entrust me to be an active tool in wildlife conservation. I thoroughly enjoy my role.

Secondly, I love to put my money where my mouth is. Or maybe better stated, to support something that I believe in. I love wildlife, public access, public lands, hunter's education and the freedom to discover the natural world. Here in West Virginia, we are blessed with so much open land to explore. But in the real world, it takes money to manage programs. And for someone like me who hunts in many states every year, I am proud to say I gladly pay for the license and the privilege.

Humans have been hunting and gathering food since the beginning of time. As a group of people who grew up in the Appalachian Mountains, it is simply in our DNA to hunt.

Lastly, an answer I find to be sometimes seen as a touchy subject is for the challenge of the sport. The adventure of chasing a mature Tom turkey or fooling a wise, old buck is downright thrilling. It is no means the only reason most of us hunt but accepting the challenge adds some spice to the dish.

Perhaps just like our ancestors, truly bringing home dinner is a wonderful delight especially when shared with people you love.

As with most things, maybe looking at the simple answer is the best. I hunt because, that is who I am.

TURKEY HUNTING IS A GIFT

This spring will be my 22nd season of chasing turkeys. I have had the pleasure of being there when a first timer gets hooked on the sport and even seen old-timers well up over memories of hunters who have gone before us.

I have flat out missed, been lost, came home empty-handed, and tagged a turkey before the coffee has a chance to perk back at camp and anything and everything in between. My youth and strong legs used to think I could out walk a turkey and I was too hard-headed and thought I could outsmart them as well. I used to think I knew a great deal about the bird and how to hunt him; but the older I get the more I realize I am a brief spectator in a turkey's world. It is simply an honor and a privilege when a hunter and a gobbler get the chance to meet up close and in person.

Mostly, I have learned a great deal about myself. I have learned how to enjoy the gift of a warm spring morning, the smell of the earth coming alive sprouting delicate fiddle head ferns, the high-pitched call of spring peepers in the distance and how to really listen to the natural world.

On a crisp spring morning before the sun's rays light every corner of the world through bluebird skies, the feathered creatures of the woods are simply too excited to remain silent. The barred owl has to shout across the hill, the blue jay has to squawk at you from high within the hemlock and the gobbler simply can't resist shouting from his roost at anything loud enough to be heard. He will gobble at trains, car doors slamming, crows calling, and even humans using locator calls to mimic other birds. By not being able to keep his mouth shut, he tells the world his exact location.

Knowing your quarry's exact location seems like an unfair advantage. In the pitch-black woods of predawn it is. But once it is light enough for the gobbler to see the ground, he again becomes the master of his woodlot. If he sees you coming, he can simply pitch out of the tree, leaving your aching legs and burning lungs longing for the truck and some eggs at the diner.

If he doesn't see you and flies down with his pack of girlfriends, the ladies who have keen enough eyes will tell Mr. Big that some fool is peering at him from behind the big white oak.

Most often than not, you will find yourself alone on ridge realizing it is probably time to go home and admit defeat. Turkeys greatest attribute is to make hunters second guess their choices and to make even the most seasoned hunters humbled to the point of laughter by a simple-minded bird.

Every turkey you manage to fool into coming within shotgun range should be counted as a gift. As I get older, I cherish those gifts more and more.

DAD'S PHEASANT

To the left of the fireplace, on the wall of the house where I grew up, was a mounted ring-necked pheasant. As unusual looking as the bird was, unlike any bird I had seen in the wild, the fact that my father had an animal mounted in the living room made the bird's allure even greater. In fact, it was the only piece of taxidermy in my childhood home.

The story told to me was simple. My father traveled to Pennsylvania on a pheasant hunting trip. And upon his return, a bird dog named Daisy and an Ithaca 16-guage shotgun were immediately purchased. After several training sessions for both dog and dad, a trip was planned. The trip resulted in one point, one flush and one dead bird.

The result of the hunt was preserved and hung on a wall in the family room. The mounted ring-necked pheasant is as much a part of my childhood as my kindergarten teacher.

I would not understand the complete fascination my father held for the bird until later in my life. For the past several seasons, a group of friends and I meet in South Dakota for a weekend of pheasant hunting. It is there, that the story of my father's hunt and his mounted game bird get freshened in my memory.

On the rolling hills directly off the Missouri River, where the South Dakota grasslands meet the farmlands, is where we hunt pheasants. We spread out in a line and walk the fields slowly as the bird dogs wag their tails and sniff the wind in front of us making their way through the brushy cover.

The scene is quiet and calm until the flush of a ring-neck pheasant pierces the windy air with the shrill of beating wings and series of loud, excited two-note calls as it bursts from the cover. It is then, someone will exclaim, "Rooster!" At that precise moment, things become lively and the art of wingshooting comes in to play.

After the report of a shotgun fills the air, the dogs begin to excitedly to search for the downed bird. Once found, the gun dog takes the bird to the hunters while in a full-blow, tail-hind-end-wiggle kind of trot. I am certain I saw the dogs smile several times with a mouthful of feathers.

I return each fall to South Dakota to watch the gun dogs work, the thrill of being close to flushing pheasant and of course, to recall memories of my father and his stories—especially the one about his dog and the mounted pheasant on our wall.

A SIMPLE LITTLE SQUIRREL HUNT

The forecast was calling for snow turning to rain. "Oh, great," I thought. I had been planning this hunt for a couple of weeks now. It was a simple little hunt, but one I had promised to myself, my brother, my son and of course my dog. I had to go despite the forecast.

The evening before the hunt, we were supposed to get one to three inches of snow but the hunting day was forecasted to be warming with a chance of late evening rain. So, with bags packed, I hit the pillow expecting the worst.

However, the first rays of daybreak showed a completely different reality. When my dog jumped into the backseat of my truck, the sun broke loose to reveal clearing skies. It was warming fast and all I could think was that the game animals were going to be moving on a day as pretty as this one.

My brother beat us to the farm and decided to hunt for sheds and to see if he could find any active squirrels. That's the thing I've learned about hunting squirrels in the winter, it is all about the weather and finding den trees. They won't be far from their dens and they don't wander far.

I unhooked Boogie's lead and turned him loose to run. After a couple of hours of being in the truck, he hunted hard. He sniffed the wind, looked up in the tree's canopy and even stopped to listen for movement. It seemed like only a couple of minutes when Boogie stood leaning against a mammoth oak tree and threw his head back and barked. When we got to the tree, Boogie was barking and wagging his tail so fast I couldn't help but feel his excitement.

"Boogie says there is a squirrel up there somewhere," I shouted over the barking. Just then, the squirrel came running down a massive limb and jumped to the neighboring tree's crown of limbs and swiftly ran in a hole in the bole of the tree. Three jumps and one short run and the squirrel was in its den.

"Wintertime squirrel hunting," I mumbled under my breath.

As the day warmed almost to t-shirt warmth, so did the hunting. For the next three hours, our hunting party acted as one team with the dog being the leader. On a bonus day in the winter, I experienced the best day of squirrel hunting I had all season long.

I'm sure glad I kept my promise to take them hunting. It was a simple little day afield but one I will remember for many seasons to come.

THEY TOOK ME ALONG

Fishing for trout played a significant role in my youth. At first I was simply a bystander. But it didn't take long before I was handed a rod and told to fish over there awhile. Why? Maybe it was because I was annoying them, maybe out of pity or maybe just to give someone a break from babysitting me, I don't know why. Why they did it doesn't matter. It's what they did that matters. They took me along on their fishing trip and I got to fish.

I recall the precise moment and the exact location when I was first handed a rod. I remember the way the cork handle felt in my hands. I remember the way the hook swayed and bobbed on the end of my line as I walked away. I even remember how hard it was to cast the line into the water with the wind blowing. But remembering all those details doesn't even come close to the memory of the tug and strain of a fish on the end of the line. My line, my rod, my fish.

With a slimy, cold fish in my little hands I walked back towards the family. Grandad noticed me first and came to inspect my catch. His reaction was equal to mine and we both beamed with pride as we called to everyone and held up the trout for all see.

West Virginia is blessed with so much water to fish.

And with a road map and the help of the WVDNR, finding cold trout waters is simple.

In my mind, there are four kinds of trout waters— wild trout streams, stocked streams, native trout streams and lakes. And since I was a child, my desire to explore as much of these waters as possible still endures.

Each type of trout water is unique and calls for a different mindset to fish. For example, lake fishing for stocked trout can be for the most part a sedentary sport. Sure, some lakes are large enough where a boat can be effective, but most lakes are fished from the bank. The strategy is to cast into the lake and wait until a hungry fish swims by and takes your bait. I have found lake fishing for trout very productive.

WVDNR stocked streams require walking and wading while casting lures, artificial and natural baits. We are blessed to have so many stocked streams.

Wild trout streams and native brook streams are the waters that haunt me the most. Trout waters filled with either brown trout that grew up there from Trout Unlimited stocking of fingerlings or wild brook trout waters are worth the time and energy scouting and finding how to unlock their mysteries. When the bugs start flying around, you will find me knee deep in them as much as possible casting flies in hopes a trout will rise.

BECOMING A FLY-FISHERMAN

The note simply said, "Nice to have the next generation of Ellis' up for a day on the water." The note was from a landowner of a farm known for its stunning mountain setting and pristine cold waters. In those waters are trout of all sizes. And if you are talented at fly-fishing and have not used all your luck at poker or life, you may meet one of the full-grown trout calling those waters home.

I was first introduced to the creek nearly twenty years ago, when my brother and I owned an outfitter service. We would assist folks in finding the best place for a get-away, or the perfect stretch of river for a family float trip. But what we really liked to do is teach people to fly-fish.

I have been blessed many times watching a true beginner leave the class with enough knowledge and passion to have a new lifetime hobby. Helping someone new to the sport is worth all the time and energy it takes untangling knots, spooking fish and wrangling fly hooks out of trees.

So, when my son asked if I could guide him on a creek in hopes of catching a trout, I was tickled. On one of the prettiest creeks I know, my son stepped into the cold water and began the process of casting a fly. I watched as he prepared his line and fly for the cast. I was anxiously waiting to see if all his backyard practice and muscle memory of casting the rod would serve him well.

With a few false casts of his line to ensure he had enough distance so that the fly would drift naturally in front of the trout, he pointed his rod towards the target and released the fly. With a mend of his line, I witness a young angler lift his rod tip towards the sky and was treated to the gift all fly-fishermen dream of—a tight line with a tiny hook holding on to a frisky trout.

As the battle played out before me, I slid down the bank into the cold water to net his catch. After a quick photo, we slid the fish head first into the current to return to his world.

With cold feet and glowing faces, we walked the path back to the truck discussing plans of fishing trips in our future. He can now call himself a fly-fisherman.

HUNTING DOGS

Maybe it's my rural upbringing or it could be that my wife is correct and I am just a big kid—either way, I love dogs. I am not particularly fond of the little fluffy dogs that the Hollywood celebrities carry around like dolls. I like working and hunting dogs.

I recall vividly my first squirrel hunt. I was too small to carry a gun but that didn't matter. I was introduced to Jip and it was love at first sight. She was a mixed breed hound that loved chasing squirrels. Jip and I were instant buddies.

A little later in life, I was introduced to a young Brittany pup. My hunting mentor had purchased her as a grouse-hunting dog and I was invited to tag along on her early training sessions. We trained and learned together all summer. I was present when she pointed her first grouse and also invited to the meal that followed shortly after her successful rookie season. I was her biggest fan.

And then I met Patch. On a crisp autumn day, I accepted an invitation to join a few friends on a turkey hunt. Being new to the sport, I was curious and eager to see how things were going to play out. It didn't take Patch long to introduce me to the game. In a narrow beech tree hollow with a drain of a creek running through it, I placed my hands on a turkey and held it up for the world to see. When Patch circled back to the scene, it appeared that she was even more excited to see the turkey than I was. I patted her head and thanked her for her efforts. It would be the first of many times I gave her thanks.

On my first trip to Africa I met Nimrod, a Rhodesian Ridgeback mix. It was his job to assist you if and when you needed help. Nimrod's specialty was tracking and his demeanor was what made him shine—he was as laid back as any hunting dog I have ever met and made a wonderful companion.

If a dangerous game animal needed bayed until the hunters could arrive, Nimrod was thrilled to do that too. Nimrod made my trip to Africa even more special and I think of him often.

I have witnessed many working dogs over my career. Beagles chasing rabbits, Catahoula curs baying hogs, Blueticks bawling at the base of tree with a raccoon peering down at them, Labs watching the sky for falling ducks, English Setters locked stiff pointing quail—all have added to the experience of a day afield.

Maybe the reason I like hunting dogs so much is for the simple fact that they seem to love the sport of hunting as much as I do. Then again, my wife may be right—I might just be the biggest kid you have ever met.

BROTHERS

My brother and I have hunted Thanksgiving week together since we were children. In fact, when we first started I was too young to carry a gun for the first few seasons. My job back then was to sit quietly alongside him watching patiently for a buck to wander into our view. Rarely did we even see a deer.

We had received permission to hunt my grandfather's old home place by his cousin who tended the farm.

When asked where we should begin our search for deer to hunt, he would point his weathered fingers towards a ridge on the back of the farm. We were certain he was more clueless than us and only allowed us to hunt the farm out of respect for our grandfather. Nonetheless, we weren't about to let him or anyone else dampen our desire to become deer hunters.

The first few years were lean. We learned where to sit to see deer with some regularity but couldn't make the connection to an antlered deer. We considered bucks as ghosts and marveled at the hunters who met after dark at the local store dropping their tailgates to show off their trophies.

And then one year, it happened. My brother and I chose to hunt separately that day. I heard the loud crack of a gunshot. I couldn't sit on a stand any longer without knowing the outcome, so I walked briskly to our meeting spot at the gate.

As dusk fell and the cold air came rushing across the ridges, I could see the dim light of his headlamp approaching. His face was radiant as he told the story of his first buck. We now were hunters—real hunters who returned home with more than cold feet and worn out legs. We hung the deer in the barn and rushed home to tell our family of our accomplishment.

But it wasn't until I put my hands on the antlers of a buck of my own did I really understand the magnitude of emotions. The following year, I sat on a small knob overlooking a grassy flat. Looking down on the flat, I saw a deer feeding towards me several hundred yards away. As he got closer, I could see his antlers. A buck was walking my way and I was well, coming unglued.

I shut my eyes to try to contain the raw energy that was causing my hands to shake and my stomach to knot. When the trigger broke, I jerked my head to see my first buck folded on the flat. I couldn't breathe, let alone walk. I had taken my first buck and when I finally put my hands on his antlers, I still couldn't believe it was true.

This past Thanksgiving week, I got to recall those feelings again as I watched my son steady his rifle and try and calm his nerves as a buck walked into range. After the well-placed shot, we walked down to see his first buck. I watched him knowing exactly the emotional connection to the natural world that was flowing through his veins. As we bent down to touch the antlers, I closed my eyes and gave thanks.

MEMORIAL DAY

There's something about May in the mountains. It's a feeling you get when you look across the hills and see every shade of green. It's the feeling you get when a day starts cool and ends warm. It's the unpredictable spring weather, with thunderstorm filled fronts that yo-yo the temperatures and the water levels in the streams that causes us to carry a raincoat and a pullover when we choose to wander outdoors. Whatever it is about May, it makes me want to be outside.

This past week, I just had to be outside. I decided to fish regardless of the weather. The targeted species was trout. I decided to harness the energy and excitement of a couple of 11-year olds as I knew they wouldn't complain about going fishing when the forecast called for heavy rains.

The plan was simple; fish after school until dark. Promptly at 4:13pm, we arrived to find the creek running high and somewhat off-color. That was the semi-good news. The bad news—the skies were getting ready to unleash a down pour that clears ditches of leaves and gravel, makes people remember to buy new wiper blades and causes basements to leak.

The off-color water provided some challenges, not to mention the finicky fish and short attention spans of young boys who had been cooped up in classrooms all day. But catching fish wasn't the point. The smell of water falling over rocks, the feel of loose earth under my feet and the sounds of excited song birds chirping their way through a lazy afternoon is a dosage of therapy that heals the scars of winter's grip.

There is simply nothing like May in West Virginia. These hills provide the perfect backdrop and always welcome us back home when we stray. The Great Seal of West Virginia contains the state's motto "Montani Semper Liberi", (Mountaineers are Always Free) and the month of May always reminds me to remember the ones who went on before me to provide it.

Tomorrow is the last Monday in May. It's a day celebrated every year by honoring those who died while serving in the military. I hope you too enjoy the freedoms they provided us by celebrating the best way sportsmen know how—by being outside in nature and giving thanks to those who gave the ultimate sacrifice in the service of their country. May we keep the sacrifices of the brave men and women of our military in our thoughts and prayers—that's who I'll be thinking about while I'm fishing.

A GIFT TURKEY

It was the luckiest turkey hunt I have ever been on. In fact, looking back at it now, I still can't believe it turned out that well. Compared to most of my hunts over my roughly 30-year career, the successful hunt last week was a textbook dream come true hunt indeed.

Perhaps I should set the tone for what a regular, run-of-the-mill day of spring gobbler hunting is like. First of all, there is always a "where's Waldo" moment during one of my turkey hunts. Call it Murphy's Law, or bad luck, but I can't deny that something weird almost always crawls into a turkey hunt with me.

Things like flat tires, dead truck batteries and alarm clock malfunctions don't even make me breathe hard anymore. I take them with a grain of salt. I have almost come to expect them.

During the hunt when nutty things unexpectedly happen is what drives me bonkers. Like the time a tree fell in the exact direction the gobbler was coming from. The coyote (multiple times now) who decides the exact moment when the gobbler is almost within shooting distance is when he should walk right out in the open and show his magnificence. Or the bobcat, which is rarely seen up close, decides today of all days it would be cool to grace you with his presence and walk close enough to you to give you the willies. I will not even mention deer or cows—they are real party-poopers.

I have enough troubles from the turkeys. I don't need any help from farm vehicles, other animals, farmers, fences, gates or friends ruining my hunt. The turkeys alone can find 1,000 other ways to mess up my hunt.

But last week's hunt went way too well. In fact, I was reluctant to even talk about it to others in my turkey-hunting circle for fear that I may somehow jinx it or cause some random thing to happen like getting crushed by a meteor while talking on my cell phone.

In fact, I had a hard time telling my buddies the story for fear that they wouldn't believe me. I could see them rolling their eyes when my success story lasted three minutes. They probably thought the turkeys had finally driven me off the edge.

It wasn't until bed that night that I began to fell somewhat normal about the hunt. I played the scene over and over in my head—owl hoot, gobble. Gobble on the roost. Get set up just off wood's road leading to gobbling. They fly down, gobble, and make a call, then gobble. Short time later, he presents himself in an area for an open shot in the hardwoods. At 7:00 am the turkey is successfully checked in electronically and I drive home.

I literally didn't know what to do with the rest of my morning and I could not have been happier. Maybe my turkey hunting luck has changed. Please don't tell the turkeys I said that.

ELK RIVER MOM

Mom dropped me off at the Smith's grocery store parking lot. I had three dollars in my pocket and a fishing rod in my hand. "I will be back at dinner time to pick you up. Be careful and promise me you won't cross the river," she said, as I shrugged at her while walking away. Somehow in my adolescent mind I thought it was all right to lie to your parents if you pretended you didn't hear them. Besides, I wasn't certain I was going to cross the shoals or not; it depended on how the fish were biting.

I sat on the coin-operated car in front of the store waiting for my friend Joe. Joe and I had been friends since the first day we meet back in third grade and had fished this set of shoals nearly everyday that summer.

The first order of business was bait. The bait would determine the type of fish we would fish for. If the water in the river was high and muddy, we would buy corn from the store and fish the backwaters for carp.

If the waters were running clear, and Joe was able to steal enough minnows from the minnow trap behind his uncle's trailer, we would fish for smallmouth and walleyes. If Mom didn't throw out the Cool Whip container full of backyard night crawlers, we might elect to sit in the shade under the sycamore tree and bottom fish for drums.

If it was too hot for everything else, we would buy livers and cross the river to the deep, shady hole behind the bridge pillar to fish for catfish. That is, after we watched Mom cross the bridge slowly five or six times trying to catch me in a lie.

We were free for the afternoon to explore the cool waters and talk as adults. On that stretch of river I learned about girls, cars, fish and most importantly life. I learned how to catch fish, where to hang my wet clothes and the true meaning of the word "friend."

On a recent flight from Detroit to Charleston the airline attendant informed us that we were making our initial approach into Charleston as the sound of the landing gear lowered. I opened the shade and peered through the little window. The plane finally straightened its path and I could see a river far below. I knew the river well. In fact, I saw the small grocery store and the set of shoals my friend and I waded and fished almost everyday that memorial summer. As I scanned the shoals for fishermen, I had a strange feeling that I was not the only one looking down on the river.

This week my Mother would have celebrated her 65th birthday. I think of her often, especially when the sounds of rippling waters and the smell of summer fill my senses.

BOY'S DAY OUT HUNTING

Written on the refrigerator calendar were the words, "Boys Day Out." To a 7 year-old, the meaning of those words caused much anticipation and excitement. Plans were drawn and strategies were discussed and eventually the day came.

The day started early with his choice of breakfast menu items. After all, it was his day so he got to choose how it started. When his body and mind were fueled, he was ready for an expedition only rivaled by Hemingway in search of the spiral-horned antelope of Africa.

His plans were concrete and simple. On his list included planting apple trees, shooting his BB gun, and stalking after the great game animals. The vehicle was packed tightly with all the supplies needed to carry out such a plan. The road to the farm was somehow different on this day, his day. The windows were down and I drove much slower than usual as we discussed the world's events man to man.

The one topic that gave him great pride and even caused him to grin at himself was simply titled, "Boys day out...No women, no drama."

As we entered the farm's gate, he threw his seatbelt off and began scanning the woods for animals only a young boy's imagination could dream of. According to his itinerary, the tree planting should come first. At the edge of a small field, we sat on the tailgate as he painstakingly marked the exact spot for each tree within his orchard. The labor required with planting trees turned his mind quickly to the next item on the list, shooting his BB gun.

After months of having to adhere to schedules from teachers, coaches, and other adults a BB gun and a jug full of BB's was a new found freedom. He started by warming up on the 25-yard target, and then set his sights on more fun things to shoot at like old stumps, dirt clods, and the occasional Grizzly that stepped out of the hardwoods.

Without having to ask permission, he proudly announced, "I'll meet you down at the river." I stood watching him as he put his BB gun in the truck and began to walk down the road. He had broken lose from adult supervision and he was proud to be walking alone.

I found him playing in a ditch line with clay stuck all over his shoes, pants, and somehow combed through his hair. With immense pride he looked up, not at all worried about being in trouble for looking like a mud turtle, and said, "Told you I would meet you at the river."

As the sun lowered in the sky, we headed back home once again driving slowly. This time the truck's cab had the satisfied sound of snoring from a young man after a long "Boys Day Out."

POP'S FLAG

My grandfather flew an American flag in his yard. It was the first thing I noticed every time we pulled in his driveway. My brother and I would be cramped into the back seat of the family car and when it came to a stop, we would fling open the doors and run as fast as we could for Pop's door. I can still hear the flag snapping in the wind and can see its bright colors against the summer's blue sky. That flag was part of my childhood and the memories of summers with him.

I never recall asking him why he flew the flag and I have no memories of him ever talking about it. I never saw it in ill repair. Whether it was our annual week with him in the summer, Thanksgiving or a visit to watch a football game, it was something that was always just there.

Everyone in town knew my grandfather was a decorated WW II veteran and an avid outdoorsman. Like the flag, there were things in his house that he never really talked about but were also always there. A shadow box in the den full of medals, a photo album in the basement filled with grainy old pictures of him and his time in the service and in the spare bedroom closet was an old chest. As a curious child, I wanted desperately to learn more but never had the nerve to ask. I couldn't understand how the family could gather for days and how not so much as a mention of the treasures would be mentioned.

My grandfather told me one day he wanted to show me something that he wanted me to have when I was ready. When all of the family was resting comfortable on the back porch with their bellies full of hamburgers and kielbasa sausages, we retreated to the spare bedroom.

He opened the closet door and brought the old chest from its resting place to the middle of the room. He went through each item and told stories behind them. There was a map outlining his infantry division's journey across Europe with all the battles highlighted. On the back of the map were signatures of all the soldiers in his unit. We spent the afternoon talking of soldiers and freedoms.

At the very end, after I swore to secrecy, he showed me an old German Luger pistol. The story behind how he obtained the pistol and the days following the event was perhaps the greatest story I have ever heard. He placed the chest back in the closet and we shook hands and returned to the family.

When I became an adult, shortly before his death, he presented me with chest containing the Luger pistol. I will in turn, tell his story and the secret of the pistol to my son one day. Until then, the Luger will have a special place in the gun safe and an American flag will fly from my house. Both represent the freedoms my grandfather held so dearly. So dearly in fact, no one ever asked him why he flew the American flag in his yard. They just knew.

GETTING OLDER

I must be getting old. I hate to admit it or even think about it but I couldn't help it when I was packing for an upcoming hunting trip. Thoughts of worry snuck into my brain about goofy things like toilet paper and which boots to pack. I never used to worry about my feet getting cold and nature is full of toiletries if you simply take the time to look. What happened to the days when rubber boots with steel shanks were extreme cold weather gear and if you thought your feet might get cold you threw on another pair of tube socks?

In anger I stuffed a pair of ultra dry, waterproof, 2000 grams of insulation, thermal lined, bomb proof, expensive, serrated cleat soled boots in my suitcase. That is, just before I stuffed an extra pair of merino wool socks in the boots as a backup, just in case.

Perhaps getting older means you don't like to be inconvenienced. Like many hunters, I like to carry a daypack in the woods with me. My suspicions of becoming old were quite evident when I decided to lighten my load a little and clean out the old daypack.

You could imagine the shear shock when I laid out its contents on the kitchen table only to find I had collected 12 hand warmers, 6 snack cakes, 2 compasses (one old school, one digital), a solar blanket, first aid kit, 67 zip ties, grunt tube, 3 Sharpies, 2 fire starters, baby wipes, a roll of toilet paper, 4 carabiners, 2 knives, a paperback book and a walkie talkie.

I have to admit, it had been a while since I gave the pack a thorough cleaning but who carries that much stuff and where is my flashlight? (Thoughts of a recent turkey hunt in Texas, sitting alone for hours in the pitch-black dark waiting for my ride, should have been enough to remember to find my flashlight but memory loss is another sign of getting old.)

My grandmother's purse had less stuff in it and she carried the same one for 20 years. If the survivor folks on TV carried in that much stuff, we would call them fakes. It is official; I am getting old.

I decided to pack the bare essentials and simply forget all that useless gear. In fact, I took out the ultra boots and instead I packed the Bean Boots I have had since college. They might not be insulated but I was determined to get back to the basics. "When I was younger, I didn't need all that gear," I said to myself. "Besides, I never get cold or lost." As soon as the words left my lips, it hit me. On second thought, perhaps I am not getting older, simply more experienced.

I decided to go with the warm boots and take along everything I had just taken out of my daypack. Just in case.

HUNTING SEASON

In case you were wondering, it is hunting season. I know everyone's schedule gets pretty full with life's responsibilities, so I thought it would be a nice service to educate the public on how to determine hunting season has arrived without the use of a calendar.

The first clue is the absence of activity on your street or in your neighborhood. Next door you may notice a lack of yard maintenance, newspapers piling up on the walk, and no cars in the driveway. A veteran hunter will spend any and all leisure time afield leaving way before daylight and returning well after dark. Don't be fooled by thinking they are out of town or on vacation, it is simply hunting season.

The second sign is camouflage. Outdoorsman will begin to wear it proudly as their uniform for the season. Ole Jim might wear his camo hat year round, but he will not break out the full attire until the season officially arrives. You can generally tell an experienced hunter from a novice by the style of camo worn. If you see someone sporting the latest fashion pattern, and it all matches, you have a rookie or someone with a rich grandmother. Generally a seasoned hunter will have a blend of patterns, slightly worn and a tad faded, but comfortable and field proven.

Next, lawn ornaments will begin to appear in backyards across the towns and ridges. These ornaments come in two common designs. The first looks like a box and will have some sort of target attached to the front. It is common to see aluminum arrows sticking out of one side of the box. The second will resemble a deer. The deer lawn ornament will have huge antlers (Typically, one of the antlers will be broken off by the kids or chewed on by the dogs.) and his eyes will be wide open. The reason he looks frightened is hunters will be practicing shooting arrows into him to tune their archery skills.

Finally, don't be alarmed if you see a group of outdoorsmen huddled around the back end of a pickup at the local convenience store. Simply walk in and get your sundries and don't pay them much attention. The more people's curiosity tempts them into looking in the truck bed, the longer they will stay. Their wives won't expect them until after dark anyhow.

I hope these simple tips will help you become more informed about the Mountain State's number one pastime and the greatest time of the year for sportsmen—hunting season.

GOOSE

There are days that sportsmen anticipate the entire year—the first day of buck season, bow season opener, or perhaps bear season. It's what helps us survive office jobs, tax collectors, and feeding hunting dogs.

This particular day was not one of those days. A phone call from a friend with a boat and I was included in a hometown adventure—a bonus day. A bonus day is the equivalent of finding a 20-dollar bill in a pair of washed jeans and should be treated as such. I was happy to simply be a part of it and no trace of it could be found on my calendar.

The blue ink of my signature on the duck stamp hadn't even had a chance to dry when the truck pulled onto the gravel road. The tires crunched the gravel as we pulled down to the river's edge. It was a warm September day and the river was running low and clear beneath blue bird skies—it was simply, "Almost Heaven."

We had set out to float a remote section of river with the hopes of finding a place or two to stop and call to some geese. I had no clue what the day would bring and even better, I didn't really care. It was someone's grand idea to throw in a couple of fishing rods just in case the geese were smarter than us and weren't in the mood to be called to.

Several miles into the trip the fishing rods came in handy. Apparently the geese didn't care much for our honks, clucks and moans but the smallmouth bass sure did.

There I was in the middle of a waterfowl hunt catching some of the biggest bass of the season. I had managed to stuff a few soft plastic baits in my shotshell bag and I barely had enough line spooled on my reel to cast far enough from the boat to be effective.

As we rounded a bend in the river, a shoal presented itself. With no geese in sight, we drifted into an eddy and let the swirling waters act as an anchor to hold the boat still as the warm summer waters floated past us. The morning sun warmed our smiling faces and it occurred to me that this day had turned from a bonus day to a day I must write on my calendar as an annual event. It's risky to try and predict the unpredictable, but I was having too much fun not to try and mirror the day again in the upcoming years. With the thought fresh in my mind, a chunky smallmouth bass took the plastic fluke lure deep into the current and began his nosedive towards the river's bottom. After several long runs, he presented himself to the side of the boat as I grinned for a picture or two.

GRANDAD'S LAST FISH

With spring flowers in full bloom, my mind drifts easily back to the springtime of my youth. Many early spring days of my youth were spent in the mountains with friends and family wading creeks and catching trout. The trips into the National Forest started as family affairs but as I got older, and a license to drive, it didn't take much of an excuse to point the truck to the mountains loaded down with trout rods and a cooler.

In all those memories, some of the fondest ones are of fishing with my grandfather.

Grandad worked in a plant where they manufactured electric conduit and spent his entire career fixing things. He spent his entire life fixing things because he was great at it and he loved helping people. As much as he was known for fixing just about anything, he was known even more as a fisherman. No matter where we went together or what we were doing around town, people always asked him about fish, tackle, baits and fishing tips.

Grandma used to tell us grandkids a story of our grandfather's passion. In her story, Grandad would work overtime all week until Friday afternoon. Then he would rush home and grab his gear and a sack dinner. He would spend all evening and night searching the water's edge of creeks for soft-shell crawdads. Toting a carbide lamp and a bait can, he would hunt for the bait. Being a fisherman, he understood the importance of bait. Not just having it, but having the absolute right bait for the right time.

There were many stories around the family and the community of Grandad catching a trophy smallmouth bass—his favorite fish on the planet. Only Grandma and her grandkids knew the whole story and the bait he used.

On a warm day earlier this week, the smells of spring brought to mind a family fishing trip many years ago. In the heart of my recollection, Grandad and I were fishing a run of a small trout stream together. I paused to watch the old man's body struggle to cast to the place his mind told him there would be a trout holding.

As my brother walked around the bend into view of us, Grandad lifted his rod and the familiar scene of bent rod and tight line attached to a fish played out before us. Grandad was in no hurry to land the fish while two impatient adolescent boys, paced the waters with nets outstretched. With fish in hand, Grandad smiled at us as the spring sun lit our faces.

Recalling the mental picture of Grandad and the last fish he ever caught is a memory I look forward to every spring when the sun warms my face. Thank you Grandad for taking me fishing.

HEADING TO THE MOUNTAINS

It's that time of year when children of all ages think about spring and remote places to relax. Growing up on Elk River, my dreams of the perfect spring break were the Monongahela Forest and the getting lost in the "mountains."

The vastness, the beauty, and the mountain air—all were exciting and could be found in the forest. But to be honest, fishing for trout was the star of the show and main draw for me.

So, when a note passed across my desk from the Forest Service about one of my favorite places on earth, I simply had to share it.

Whether you are an avid trout angler in pursuit of those colorful and elusive native brookies, the weekend angler seeking a high quality fishing experience, or a visitor just traveling through the area, the Monongahela National Forest is for you!

The Monongahela is home to 87 species of fish including a wide variety of game fishes and associated non-game fish. With more than 900,000 acres of National Forest System lands that range in elevation between 1,425 feet and 4,863 feet, the Monongahela offers a diversity of freshwater

fishing experiences for everyone. You will find an
assortment of aquatic habitats to explore and enjoy
in the hundreds of miles of mountain streams and
the more than 250 acres of man-made lakes on the
Forest.

The Monongahela National Forest features
more than 600 miles of coldwater streams that are
inhabited year-round by native brook trout. These
streams are prized for the vital habitat they provide
in sustaining West Virginia's only native trout. In
addition, some trout streams on the Forest have
become home to non-native rainbow and brown
trout populations that are now wild and naturally
reproducing.

Approximately 350 miles of stream on the
Forest provide seasonal trout waters that transition
exclusively into cool or warm water fisheries in
summer. Many of these streams are stocked during
the fall, winter, and spring with hatchery raised
rainbow, golden rainbow, brown, and brook trout
by the West Virginia Division of Natural Resources
to provide put-and-take trout fishing opportunities.
The warm water angler will especially enjoy honing
their skill in streams such as the South Branch
Potomac River and the Greenbrier River that offer
some of the State's best smallmouth bass waters.

Those that enjoy the relaxing tranquility of lake
fishing will want to experience the 251 acres of man-
made lakes that are distributed among 4 reservoirs
nestled in the mountains across the Forest. Bass,

bluegill, catfish, and trout are fair game for those that wish to explore the water's depth beneath the mirrored images cast upon these lakes.

Whether it is trout or bass, lakes or streams, you are sure to discover your fishing interests on the Monongahela National Forest.

Thanks for the note and the trip down memory lane. I appreciate it greatly and just marked a few days on my calendar—"trout fishing in the mountains."

ABOUT THE AUTHOR

Chris is an outdoor-industry veteran who has worked with some of its largest and most iconic companies, launching new products and building awareness. He has also been a member of startup teams that have built new brands from concept to proven product.

In addition, he is a weekly outdoor columnist for the *Beckley Register-Herald* and the *Huntington Herald-Dispatch*.

Chris is a passionate and lifelong outdoorsman, who has hunted all over the world. Chris prefers to prowl his hillside farm in West Virginia, with his squirrel dog Boogie or to be knee-deep in a creek in search of a rising trout. He is also hopelessly afflicted by the lure of the wild turkey, and with no cure in sight, has submitted to the addiction.

Made in the USA
Coppell, TX
19 June 2021

57717924R00075